MARINA WARNER

SIX MYTHS OF OUR TIME

Marina Warner was born in London to an Italian mother and an English father. She is the author of a collection of stories, *The Mermaids in the Basement*, and four novels, the most recent of which is *Indigo; The Lost Father* (1988) was a Regional Winner of the Commonwealth Writers' Prize. She also writes history and criticism, focusing mainly on female symbolism (*Alone of All Her Sex; Joan of Arc; Monuments and Maidens*). She is the editor of *Wonder Tales*, a collection of fairy tales by the great women storytellers of the seventeenth and eighteenth centuries, and author of a study of the fairy tale, *From the Beast to the Blonde*, both of which are forthcoming. She has recently been made visiting Professor of Women's Studies at the University of Ulster.

ALSO BY MARINA WARNER

SIX MYTHS
OF OUR TIME

SIX MYTHS

OF OUR TIME

Little Angels, Little Monsters,

Beautiful Beasts, and More

MARINA WARNER

VINTAGE BOOKS

A Division of Random House, Inc.   New York

FIRST VINTAGE BOOKS EDITION, FEBRUARY 1995

Library of Congress Cataloging-in-Publication Data
Warner, Marina, 1946–
[Managing monsters]
Six myths of our time : little angels, little monsters, beautiful beasts, and more / Marina Warner.
p. cm.
Originally published under title: Managing monsters.
London: Vintage, 1994.
Includes bibliographical references.
ISBN 0-679-75924-7
1. Myth.   2. Popular culture—Great Britain.
3. Civilization, Modern—1950–   I. Title.
BL313.W37   1995
824'.914—dc20   94-38915
CIP

Book design by Mia Risberg
Author photograph © Jerry Bauer

Manufactured in the United States of America
10 9 8 7 6 5 4 3 2 1

For

Conrad, Laurence, and Julian

With Much Love

And all the little monsters said in a chorus:
You must kiss us.
What! You who are evil,
Ugly and uncivil.
You who are cruel,
Afraid and needy,
Uncouth and seedy.

Yes, moody and greedy.
Yes, you must bless us.

But the evil·you do,
The endless ado.
Why bless you?
You are composed of such shameful stuff.

Because, said the monsters, beginning to laugh,
Because, they said, cheering up.
You might as well. You are part of us.

Suniti Namjoshi
St. Suniti and the Dragon

CONTENTS

ACKNOWLEDGEMENTS

I was helped in conversations and references throughout the writing of these lectures, and I thank all my sources—friends, colleagues, family. Sue Slipman, Peter Hulme, Roy Foster read certain lectures beforehand—to them my gratitude for their comments. Ruth Padel, Malcolm Jones, Lisa Appignanesi, Jan Nederveen Pieterse, and Peter Dronke were an especial inspiration. Elizabeth Burke produced the series for the BBC; she was a highly challenging first audience, and I owe her a very great deal. To John Dewe Mathews, who put up with disruption and despair, much thanks, too.

FOREWORD

This sequence of short essays on contemporary mythology was written in the autumn of 1993 as six half-hour radio talks in the BBC annual series of Reith Lectures. A British institution, like Henley regatta, cream teas, and pantomime dames, the lectures were founded in 1948 in memory of Lord Reith, the architect of the BBC and shaper of its idea of public broadcasting; to him, communications were as fundamental a part of society as law or parliament; concomitantly, the people who wielded power in this domain were responsible, like lawgivers and lawmakers, to the common culture, both intellectual and civic. The Corporation—or the Beeb, as it came to be known—was a public, independent instrument of the people who listened to it and worked on it—not of government.

This was a revolutionary concept of a state entertainment service, as radical in its way as the National Health system, and it gave the BBC a historic role in the fashioning of national identity in this century, including, for example, the popularizing of the monarchy. But, like many of the country's strongest institutions (and the British constitution itself), the BBC exists as folk memory, a kind of orally transmitted legend full of spirited idealism and valour. This situation has led to decades of increasing turmoil and rancour, especially in the last fifteen years, as the government and the broadcasters fight over the BBC's relation to the public and to politics. Reith himself, or at least the legendary gruff, high-minded, low church Scots persona that has been handed down, epitomized the old staunch commitment to a cultural public service—as well as a certain we-know-what's-good-for-you paternalism.

The Reith lectures from the start reflected the man's values. The invitation to give them carries no brief, but it seemed to me that the founder's ghost, like Hamlet's father's, was urging, Remember me. But I was, according to the unwritten code, an odd avatar for the old bachelor and patriarch to summon. Only one woman had given the series before: Margery Perham, a historian who delivered her fine lectures of 1961, 'The Colonial Reckoning', on the future of Africa. The lapse of thirty-three years before another woman was not due to policy—or—does this really need to be said?—to lack of candidates. It was due to the invisible establishment character of the lectures—as with the Garrick Club, or the Long Room at Lord's Cricket Ground, or Eton College, or the bar of El Vino in Fleet Street during its heyday; they were simply assumed to be on the whole off limits to women.

There's no deliberate malice or open contempt in this exclusion, just that dippy, distracted, happy-go-lucky vagueness of British public life—which so often fails to take stock of what is happening until it is too late. But the effect of the exclusion meant that to be a woman giving the lectures was one of the most conspicuous tasks I could have been asked to take on: I was ipso facto representative of my sex.

When Bertrand Russell gave the first series, in 1948, they were called 'Authority and the Individual'—a title itself eloquent of confidence in the central position of the human subject. It would be an unlikely topic for anyone to choose in 1994. But he set the tone, as Reith had set the style (wisdom for the common man), and it would continue: themes like 'Science and Common Understanding' by Robert J. Oppenheimer (1953), 'Art and Anarchy' by Edgar Wind (1960), Richard Hoggart's 'Only Connect'

(1971), and Denis Donoghue's 1982 series, 'The Arts Without Mystery'. The lectures went out on the Home Service (not the 'difficult' Third Programme) and they attract, today, over a quarter of a million listeners on their first broadcast and thousands more on the repeat later the same week.

Unlike many of my male predecessors, I am a writer who works on her own, outside academe or any other institution. Writing is a private activity, pursued alone and in silence, and broadcasting in many ways is its exact opposite. But as it was an unexpected honour to be asked, as friends commanded me to stand up for women, and as the radio has inherited some of the role that storytelling used to play in communities, I decided to enter some of the most electric contemporary debates about identity—sexual, family, and national—and argue my conviction that the fictions and narratives of a society contribute as fundamentally to its character as its laws and economy and political arrangements, that the dimension of the 'imaginary' is too often overlooked in the struggles to define the nature of men, of women, of children, to express exclusion and belonging. I thought I would draw on my interest in fairy tales, legends, myths to look at how they interpenetrate and influence our lives today.

When a museum assembles scraps of a vanished civilisation to show schoolchildren how people lived, in that place, at that time, it might put on display a drinking bowl, a relief of an emperor hunting lions, a coin, the sole of a sandal, a brooch or necklace. Such material remnants reveal ways of life, interests and activities, social arrangements; but they are also likely to be eloquent of the culture's belief system. A winged being might be stamped on the coin, communicating victory, or luck, or virtue, or vengeance; the jewellery, too, might bear images of the longings and the fears of the wearer—a charm for fertility, a piece of coral against the evil eye. Belief systems naturally involve theology and metaphysics, but mythology plays its part in them as it does in what has been called, since the nineteenth century, folklore; Christians do not on the whole have a problem accepting that the feast when the saviour was born falls on a day calculated by the sun and celebrated for symbolic reasons understood and honoured long before the Christian era: the winter solstice, and the start of the new year's waxing light.

Historical research has always led me to myth; the attempt to see and hear people in the past carries investigations into areas far beyond the legal, economic and personal circumstances in which they lived, or the sequence of events in their experience. Even the most immediate and intense emotional upheavals pass through a mesh of common images and utterance which are grounded in ideas about nature and the supernatural, about destiny and origin. These are rarely empirical, more usually imaginary. Death, in every culture, is faced by means of rituals which have multiple functions, but one of them is certainly to give the bereaved a way of thinking and talking about their loss. Such rituals, even in secular and rationalist systems, have deep connections to myth. Maud Pember Reeves, when she was working on her pioneering study of the urban poor in London in the 1910s, *Round About a Pound a Week,* found that they gave a substantial portion of their pittance to the undertakers as burial insurance, so that they should not suffer a pauper's funeral. Their fear wasn't only based in anxiety about social dishonour— though this isn't to be lightly scorned—but in the need to deal with death itself in all its supernatural implications. In a family surviving on next to nothing, it counted as a necessity of life, alongside bread, alongside soap.

Religion derives from *religio,* and the word's root, from *lego,* to bind, conveys the binding effect of religious observance—belief and worship. Myths don't necessarily command faith in the same way (indeed, it's not certain that the Greeks themselves believed in their myths, in the sense that a Christian believes in the Incarnation). In common usage, the word myth rather invites dissent, implying delusion and falsehood. But my underlying premise, in these six lectures, is that myths are not always delusions, that deconstructing them does not necessarily mean wiping them, but that they represent ways of making sense of universal matters, like sexual identity and family relations, and that they enjoy a more vigorous life than we perhaps acknowledge, and exert more of an inspiration and influence than we think.

The lectures were written to be read aloud, and are only half an hour long; they aren't intended for the audience of a university conference, or the participants in a seminar. The point is to appeal broadly, so the theoretical basis of the arguments is intended to emerge by implication, as in fiction, rather than be stated openly. However, to clarify my position: my approach to myth is influenced by the French school of classicists, anthropologists and historians, notably Georges Dumézil, Jean-Pierre Vernant, Pierre Vidal-Naquet, Marcel Detienne and Nicole Loraux, who have analysed with exhilarating bravura certain stories and legends, cult practices and festivals, paying detailed attention to the way they are interwoven with social systems and how they both inform and reveal their workings; their approach is not strictly psychoanalytical, but their findings draw on psychology too to illuminate human behaviour with dazzling and valuable insight. The work amplifies and extends the Freudian interpretation of myth as a key to the inner structures of consciousness, but it differs fundamentally from both Freudian and Jungian approaches by insisting that the very meanings of stories, rituals and images change in relation to the social structure with which they interact.

I'm also indebted, as anyone who knows them will recognize, to Roland Barthes's famous essays, of 1957, *Mythologies,* and his analysis of contemporary French culture. Barthes's fundamental principle is that myths are not eternal verities, but historical compounds, which successfully conceal their own contingency and changes and transitoriness so that the story they tell looks as if it cannot be told otherwise, that things always were like that and always shall be. 'Myth,' he writes, 'transforms history into nature.' Barthes's study almost amounts to an exposé of myth, as he reveals how it works to conceal political motives and secretly circulate ideology through society. Of course I haven't succeeded in doing what he did, but even within the limits of my range, my own view is less pessimistic; I believe the process of understanding and clarification to which Barthes contributed so brilliantly can give rise to newly told stories, can sew and weave and knit different patterns into the social fabric and that this is a continuous enterprise for everyone to take part in. Ancient myths of the kind I describe, dangerous mothers, warrior heroism, are perpetuated through cultural repetition, transmitted through a variety of pathways. But this does not mean they will never fade, to yield to another, more helpful set of images or tales. The school of mythological interpretation to which I would like to belong could take as its motto the last thought of Plato's *Republic:* 'And it is thus, Glaucon, that the myth has been saved from oblivion and has not been lost. If we put our faith in it, it may even save us, ourselves.' Even after banishing the poets as liars from his ideal state, Plato resorted to a hope that stories might provide a way of salvation. The myths he recorded and preserved may not be the ones that speak to the needs of today, but his philosophy at least admits the possibility that such stories might exist.

The anthropology of Dumézil offers a very useful tripartite structure of society with which to examine myths and the ideology they encode: he divided the areas myths address into fertility (the continuation of the species, and the control of generation and children), physical power (the authority of the warrior, and sometimes the king) and sovereignty (which includes priestly authority, magic, and art). This scheme shaped my line of inquiry, into contemporary struggles for control of women and children, into current images of masculine power; and into the ways history and national identity mesh in tales of strangers, of enemies, of outsiders.

Each essay can be read on its own (the original radio audience changes from week to week), but the connections are, I hope, implicit between the themes. Like the children's party game of Pass the Parcel, I see the issue of mothers and their authority uncovering the question of men's roles; as boys and as future lovers, partners, husbands and fathers, men lead on to the issue of children and their upbringing. The threat of violence so often present in images of the male opens up the question of contemporary attitudes to humanity in its natural state. Children have offered a conventional image of this condition, symbolic of both innocence and its opposite. While I was writing about the crisis around children, a two-year-old, James Bulger, was abducted and murdered in Liverpool by two boys aged ten and eleven; this tragedy struck resonances with the public in ways that revealed how deeply children represent ideals and how his destruction mirrored a general failure.

Within the dream of innocence lies the imaginary state of

wildness: the natural realm where animals live, which savages are also thought to inhabit. Like the child, this place can hold up the image of paradise lost, or of an unruly and dangerous territory which must be ordered, tamed, even consumed. And at the hidden heart of the parcel, in the middle, beneath all the enfolded layers, there's the secret treasure: the story of identity and belonging, the myth of home, which places everyone in relation to mothers, to fathers, to offspring, to here and to elsewhere, to time past and time present—and in so doing lays the path of the future, where we may or may not be saved. It seemed to me that ethnic nationalism threatens civil harmony and the traditional tolerance of our evolving democracy more profoundly than any other contemporary story, and so I concentrated on the elements in the British historical imagination which resort to insularity to assert identity and power.

The lectures are so short that it was absurd to tackle such vast issues, I know. But stories are my theme, and, as I say, I wanted to keep the storytelling character of the radio talk. In *Invisible Cities*, Italo Calvino's novel, Marco Polo tells the Great Khan about his travels all over the world, but at one point, the Great Khan turns on the storyteller and reproaches him bitterly for telling him lies. The places Polo is describing have never existed, they're idle tales, 'consolatory fables'. To which Marco Polo answers, 'This is the aim of my explorations; examining the traces of happiness still to be glimpsed, I gauge its short supply. If you want to know how much darkness there is around you, you must sharpen your eyes, peering at the faint lights in the distance.' Stories offer glimpses for the listener to take away and develop, and the medium of radio itself offers a forum where ideas can be put across for debate. I would like to have given more account of the faint lights in the distance, to have included the work of artists, writers, teachers and thinkers who are re-shaping inherited stories to shake off stale prejudices, who are refreshing the stock of common images—and there are many of them. But the acuteness of current problems, cultural and polit-ical, as well as the restriction of the time allowed, meant that the faint lights were showing up a great amount of darkness.

SIX MYTHS
OF OUR TIME

ONE

MONSTROUS MOTHERS

Women Over the Top

Queen Victoria opened the first dinosaur theme park at Sydenham in South London in 1852. She presided over the unveiling
of twenty-nine full-scale models made by Benjamin Waterhouse
Hawkins, who was the draughtsman Darwin himself had em-
ployed to depict the animals he found on his voyage in the *Beagle*.
The word 'dinosaur'—dread lizard—had been coined in 1841
by the leading palaeontologist of the time, Richard Owen, and
Hawkins made his dinosaurs to Owen's state-of-the-art specifi-
cations.

Spick and span signs in gold and scarlet paint direct visitors
to the park today to the 'Farmyard—Boats—and—Monsters'.
Monsters, not dinosaurs: the distinction between natural history
and myth wasn't drawn then. There, on an island in a lake,

crouching under mixed plantings of large trees, the concrete creatures come into view: the pterodactyl spreads its wings like a large heron, the snout of the mosasaurus emerges from the water like the toothy maw of Jonah's whale in a medieval illumination, ichthyosaurus with daisywheel eyes seems to waddle on fins as comfortably as a walrus. Their inertia in the suburban London park is pastoral, reassuring: dinosaurs spending the afternoon at their club in St James'.

A hundred and forty years on, in a much more famous park, the dinosaurs are living, moving, crying, talking—almost—the simulations and models in *Jurassic Park* give a glow of genuine wonder to the film. But the distant past and the immediate present converge in the plot to make the primordial visible in another, metaphorical way: the dinosaurs are presented as authentic forerunners in time, scientifically accurate, but at the same time their character has evolved to embody contemporary fantasies.

The velociraptors, as they hop and scurry and pounce and give chase, suspend disbelief even in the most cynical of viewers; small, mobile, quick on their feet, hunting in pairs and even articulate, they represent rather a change from the lumbering dinosaurs of Sydenham Park. In my childhood, *Tyrannosaurus rex* was the only carnivore then taught in the classroom, and even he didn't possess the savage tenacity, nimble skills, and mental energy of these predators in *Jurassic Park*. Dinosaurs, even called monsters, seemed benign giants then, but today they've become cunning, voracious, nippy—and female.

Michael Crichton's clever plot holds much interest for students of myths today. First, femaleness, via such media as this film, is represented as the sex of origin, the scientists tell us: you have to add a Y chromosome to the original DNA to generate a male of the species. Keep it back, and life is viable, and female.

Originally grown, as everyone knows, from the DNA in blood found in a mosquito preserved in amber, the dinosaurs epitomise the chaotic natural energy of fertility governed by the secular priests of the temple of science. They were all made female so that they couldn't breed, and therefore could be controlled.

In this, the dystopic theme park mirrors our world: one of the scientists marvels, 'life found a way', when sure enough, the all-female population begins to breed—by craftily mutating some ambidextrous frog DNA. Thus female organisms, in the film, prove ultimately uncontrollably fertile, resistant to all the constraints of the men of power. The story can be reduced to a naked confrontation between nature-coded female with culture-coded male: the bristling, towering, jagged, megavolt fence cannot hold the force of the primeval at a stage of intelligent evolution. Velociraptors collaborate on the kill—one as decoy, one as executioner—and want nothing more than to snack on human flesh. It's not incidental that the final confrontation takes place between a picture-perfect nuclear family—mum, dad, boy, girl—and the two velociraptors on the rampage, and that the outcome of the feeble romantic interest is that the surviving palaeontologist decides to accept his role as a man and become the father of a family.

Is the terror the velociraptors inspire in any way connected to their femaleness? It isn't emphasised as such—though the book calls the park a matriarchy. Yet popular films of this kind often refract popular concerns in metaphorical terms, and then reinforce them. No director of the contemporary cinema rivals Steven Spielberg's ability to touch a common chord. He broke all records with the takings on *E.T.* and now, a decade later, has outstripped them with *Jurassic Park,* which has made over $900 million worldwide.

The deadly female predator prowls in many other popular artefacts, in the film *Fatal Attraction,* in Margaret Atwood's latest novel, *The Robber Bride;* the two velociraptors at the climax of *Jurassic Park* could well be called Thelma and Louise—after a bout of hellraising, there's nowhere else for the story to take them but death. All such she-monsters must in one way or another be despatched by the plot—or by the hero—as securely as any mythological dragon or monster of classical myth—preferably before they've perpetuated themselves.

The accelerating pace of change since the Fifties has magnified the influence, the power, and the dissemination of myths. As everything changes, from the political map to the distribution of wealth, as human ingenuity leads to scientific breakthroughs which offer salvation and, at the same time, destruction, as strains on the family grow, the imagination hunts for stories to explain the pervasive malaise. One of the stories in mass circulation today is a very old one, but it's taken on new vigour: women in general are out of control, and feminism in particular is to blame. It's odd to think that misogynist jokes are used to attack women for wanting to trap men into marriage. Now, the attacks run the opposite way. The tabloids bitterly quote young mothers who say, 'So who needs men?'

Feminism today has become a bogey, a whipping boy, routinely produced to explain all social ills: women's struggle for equality of choice in matters of sex, their grasp of sovereignty over their bodies, are blamed in particular for the rise in family breakdown, the increase of divorce, and the apparently spiralling delinquency and violence of children. In these lectures, I'll be looking at the mythic accretions clustering stickily to these themes. Men are no longer in control, mothers are not what they used to be, and it's the fault of Germaine Greer, *Cosmopolitan* and headlined stars who choose to be single mothers, like Michelle Pfeiffer. By holding up to the light modern mythical nodes of this kind I hope to loosen, in some cases, their binding grip on our imagination. Replying to one story with another which unravels the former has become central to contemporary thought and art—text as well as image. The idea of a kind of cultural *kontakion,* the Greek antiphonal chorus across the nave, of response and reply, invocation and challenge, opens a new angle of view. As Jessica Rabbit says, in the film about her husband, 'I'm not really bad. I'm just drawn that way.'

The she-monster's hardly a new phenomenon. The idea of a female, untamed nature which must be leashed, or else will wreak havoc, closely reflects anthropocentric and mythological encounters with monsters, in spite of the hard scientific credentials of the advisers on the film. Greek myth alone offers a host of Keres, Harpies, Sirens, Moirae. Associated with fate and death in various ways, they move swiftly, sometimes on wings; birds of prey are their closest kin—the Greeks didn't know about dinosaurs—and they seize, as in the word raptor. But seizure also describes the effect of the passions on the body; inner forces, Lussa—Madness—Ate—Folly—personified in Homer and the tragedies as feminine, snatch and grab the interior of the human creature and take possession.

Ungoverned energy in the female always raises the issue of motherhood and the extent of maternal authority; fear that the natural bond excludes men and eludes their control courses through ancient myth, which applies various remedies. In Aeschylus's *Oresteia,* when Orestes has murdered his mother, Clytemnestra, the matriarchal Furies want justice against the matricide—but they find themselves confronting a new order—led by the god Apollo. Orestes is declared innocent, in a famous resolution which still has power to shock audiences today. The god decrees:

> The mother of what's called her offspring's no parent
> but only the nurse to the seed that's implanted.
> The mounter, the male's the only true parent.
> She harbours the bloodshoot, unless some god blasts it.
> The womb of the woman's a convenient transit.

In this brutal act of legislation, the god of harmony declares that henceforward, in civilised society, only the father counts. The mother only acts as an incubator.

The urban hero, representative of his paternal lineage as well as of culture and the city, subdues elemental she-monsters like the hundred-headed Hydra or the snaky-haired Medusa with his military might, and sometimes—as in the case of Odysseus and the Sphinx—with the shamanistic insight which will win him kingship. The spectre of gynocracy, of rule by women, stalks through the founding myths of our culture: both Theseus and Hercules fight with the Amazons—and subdue their queens. The Amazons' separatist queendom made them tantalising but also monstrous in the eyes of the Greeks; the terrible massacres of their army depicted on stone reliefs and vases redounded to the fame of the Greek heroes as surely as cutting off Medusa's head.

In the folklore of the past, classical and medieval, the female beast, like the velociraptors, was sometimes cunning—and purposely concealed her true nature: the hero only learns that his beautiful lover Mélusine turns into a serpent at the weekend by peeping at her; the Sirens lured men with their deceitful songs, and later tempted fierce anchorites in the desert, approaching St Anthony, for instance, with honeyed words, hiding their diabolical

[handwritten margin note: * It was Oedipus!]

nether parts under sumptuous dresses. Male beasts, as in 'Beauty and the Beast', or male devils, as in the 'Temptations of St Anthony', don't possess the same degree of duplicity: you can tell you're dealing with the devil on the whole. But when evil comes in female guise, you have to beware: the fairy queen may turn to dust in your arms and poisonous dust at that. This is a trope that sends thrills through stories as disparate as Wagner's *Tannhäuser,* in which the knight loses his soul to the carnal goddess of the Venusberg, and Rider Haggard's *She,* where as you might remember from the film, Ursula Andress agreed to crack open like a speeded-up earthquake to reveal that in spite of the image of loveliness she presented, she's nothing but a crumbling hag. But none of these dissembling serpents and monsters can compare with Keats's vision, in his gorgeous romance noir, 'Lamia':

She was a gordian shape of dazzling hue
Vermilion-spotted, golden, green, and blue;
Striped like a zebra, freckled like a pard,
Eyed like a peacock, and all crimson barred;
And full of silver moons, that, as she breathed,
Dissolved, or brighter shone, or interwreathed
Their lustres with the gloomier tapestries . . .
She seemed, at once, some penanced lady elf,
Some demon's mistress, or the demon's self . . .
Her head was a serpent, but ah, bitter-sweet!
She had a woman's mouth with all its pearls complete . . .
Her throat was serpent, but the words she spake
Came, as through bubbling honey, for Love's sake . . .

But when Lamia woos Lycius she does not of course reveal her snaky shape and nature. Only at the last minute, at the

9

wedding feast, she's unmasked. 'And with a frightful scream she vanished'—while the poor bridegroom expires in a swoon.

The fairy seductress achieves her aims through her arts: in 'Lamia', she conjures a palace of delights straight out of *The Arabian Nights;* in the legends which inspired Keats, the temptress often lures her prey into a realm where there is no pain, no ageing, no thought of the morrow. Such fairy wives do not only make a pretence of being women; they also contradict all ideas of proper womanly conduct. Of the throng of mythical and monstrous enchantresses, one of the most famous and most fascinating of all is still Medea. Medea embodies extreme female aberration from the tragedy by Euripides in the fifth century BC to the fictional translation of her story in Toni Morrison's masterpiece, *Beloved,* published in 1987.

It is through Medea's sorcery that Jason wins the Golden Fleece: she lulls the snake its guardian with a potion obtained from Hecate, Queen of the Night. But she also uses her magic powers to cheat her father, boil an enemy in oil, cut up her brother into little pieces, and eventually, when Jason has abandoned her, to murder her two children by him. Euripides dramatised with powerful empathy Medea's tragedy: when Jason decides to take another wife more useful to his current ambitions, Medea, who after all had betrayed and killed so much on his behalf, turns on those she loves in revenge. Her maternity is the terrain of her authority—of all the authority left to her—and so she strikes at Jason where he is most vulnerable, and where his reach—and all men's—is weakest. This is the logic of her atrocity in cultural and social terms, that she perverts motherhood, because motherhood remains the principal ground of her power. Among bad mothers of fantasy she is the worst; as such she speaks to our times, when the bad mother is always present as an issue, as a threat, as an excuse, as a pleasurable self-justification and as a political argument. Women still use, and abuse, the authority they are allowed as mothers, because it is what they have, or, as in Medea's case, what they have left.

Euripides's tragedy, written in the fifth century BC, introduced Medea the child killer, and has made this side of her much more familiar than other texts, which stress her enchantments and in some cases her humanity. We pick and choose bad mothers to suit our times just as we pick our dinosaurs. Apollonius of Rhodes, two hundred years after Euripides, in *The Voyage of Argo* does not mention Medea the murderer. In his story, her crime—for which she weeps piteously—consists only in eloping with Jason and cheating her father.

But Medea the child murderer contravenes the most fundamental criterion of femininity—maternal love. She shares this with many fantasies of female evil: the inquisition condemned witches for cannibal feasts on children; in Judaic myth, the succubus Lilith was believed to haunt cradles of newborn infants to carry them off, and the classical Lamia was a child stealer as well as a bloodsucker. Amulets against these harmful powers were worn in medieval Europe; satanic cults today are held to practise the same gory rites. Myths of female aberration predispose the mind to believe in these monstrous crimes; in even more sinister fashion, they offer imaginary models for action—the new witchcraft movement models its rituals on inquisitorial manuals which synthesised the most grotesque and fearful phantasmagoria.

Myths about female monstrousness have also stirred resistance—an antiphonal response of women's voices, who have sometimes claimed the wicked heroines as foremothers, sometimes disclaimed them as slanderous fictions. In 1405, the poet and historian Christine de Pizan, one of the earliest women to support her family by writing, compiled a riposte to the circulating tittle-tattle about women in her *Book of the City of Ladies*. She set up an array of heroines, geniuses, leaders, and saints, and portrayed them building a heavenly city. Among the paragons, without turning a hair, she included Medea:

> Medea . . . was very beautiful, with a noble and upright heart and a pleasant face. In learning, however, she surpassed and exceeded all women; she knew the powers of every herb and all the potions which could be concocted . . . and she was ignorant of no art which can be known. With her spells she knew how to make the air become cloudy or dark, how to move winds from the grottoes and caverns of the earth, and how to provoke other storms in the air, as well as how to stop the flow of rivers, confect poisons, create fire to burn up effortlessly whatever object she chose and all such similar arts. It was thanks to the art of her enchantments that Jason won the Golden Fleece.

No mention of mayhem here: only a passing allusion to her ability to 'confect poisons'. Later, in a passage on the dangers of love, Pizan relates that Medea unfortunately fell in love with Jason, and listened to her passion, only to find that he abandoned her. This turned her 'despondent', writes Pizan. Again, no memory of the remarkable form Medea's despondency took.

When I first read this, nearly twenty years ago, I thought Pizan was absurdly coy, and felt that feminism could not proceed without facing women's crimes as well as their wrongs—the ills they did as well as those done to them. This is still my position—

when it comes to historical events; but with regard to myths which shape thought and action and history the question becomes much more complicated. Every telling of a myth is a part of that myth: there is no ur-version, no authentic prototype, no true account. Pizan's Medea is as mythically true as Euripides's; Pizan is important because she's one of the first women writers to tell stories against the grain of tradition. Hers might tend to whitewash; but the tradition she inaugurated tends more to accept, even revel in the darkness.

The mythical she-monster's allure spellbound Sylvia Plath, for instance. The phantom of Medea herself materialises in 'Edge', one of Plath's most troubling and potent poems, when she invokes the triple death of mother and children as if it were a female calling, meeting a need, matching a desire:

> *The woman is perfected.*
> *Her dead*
>
> *Body wears the smile of accomplishment,*
> *The illusion of a Greek necessity*
>
> *Flows in the scrolls of her toga,*
> *Her bare*
>
> *Feet seem to be saying:*
> *We have come so far, it is over.*
>
> *Each dead child coiled, a white serpent . . .*

Here Plath peels away the horror which greets the sight, to uncover the voluptuous shiver it inspires: her necrophiliac vision satisfies the worst imaginings of women's malignancy and offers at the same time an image of fitting self-punishment. Plath herself didn't make a recording of 'Edge', but in 1963, she read on the radio her 'Lady Lazarus'. In this poem, she moves through despairing, holocaust imagery to grasp its morbid power with hard and angry pleasure.

I turn and burn.
Do not think I underestimate your great concern.

Ash, ash—
You poke and stir.
Flesh, bone, there is nothing there—

A cake of soap,
A wedding ring,
A gold filling.

Herr God, Herr Lucifer
Beware
Beware.

Out of the ash
I rise with my red hair
And I eat men like air.

Plath defies her audience to deny her her transgressive appetites: nocturnal, man-eating, child-killer, she turns to fantasy and projections to increase her own powers of verbal enchantment.

Many other writers and artists and performers today have also moved onto enemy territory where Medea and other monsters are pacing: Toni Morrison, in her novel *Beloved*, dramatised an incident in her native Ohio that had taken place in the turmoil of the aftermath of the Civil War, when a slave had killed her young daughter rather than let her be taken back into slavery in the household of a brutal master. Morrison's imagination becomes itself possessed by the spirit of Sethe, the mother, and of Beloved, the child who haunts her. She brings the terrible act of infanticide so powerfully before the reader that all stock reactions burn up in the passionate intensity of her sympathy. The novel itself works like sorcery—through incantation, and conjuring of ghosts. Morrison's Medea isn't Pizan's courtly wisewoman, or Plath's demonic mistress, but distils the pure torment of a woman in the grip of a vicious history. The dedication of *Beloved,* to 'Sixty Million and more' makes explicit the work's character as a cenotaph, to the African transports in the slave trade, many of them nameless, obliterated.

Many other contemporary artists, performers, as well as writers have also seized myths of female danger. Moving in to occupy the metaphorical objects of derision and fear has become a popular strategy. Sometimes this takes the form of ironically co-opting a jibe, or even an insult—as in the open defiance of the black rock group called Niggers with Attitude, or the ironic names of women's enterprises, like the famous publishers, Virago. In Zagreb, five writers were recently denounced as dangerous women in the Croatian nationalist press: the targets immediately accepted the label, and their supporters now wear badges proclaiming them 'Opasna Žena'—a dangerous woman. This is a form of well-proven magic, uttering a curse in order to undo or claim its power, pronouncing a name in order to command its field of meaning. Former misogynist commonplaces are now being seized by women; in rock music, in films, in fiction, even in pornography, women are grasping the she-beast of demonology for themselves. The bad girl is the heroine of our times, and transgression a staple entertainment: Madonna flexing her crotch with her hand, singing 'Papa don't preach.'

But this defiance sometimes results, it seems to me, in collusion, it can magnify female demons, rather than lay them to rest, for men and for women. The limits of the carnivalesque, of turning the world upside down as a rebel strategy, have long been recognised: make the slave king for a day and he'll be docile for a year. Attaching different values to *idées fixes* about unruly women proves an ineffectual line of resistance to material problems. Madonna, as she showed in her book, *Sex,* extols her own power in wilful and mindless blindness to most women's continuing vulnerability in sexual matters: in her case, degradation is a fantasy, and she's in a unique position to choose to find it sweet. It's interesting that some of her most adoring women fans, who have recently published their dreams about her, avoid— even in their unconscious, it seems—the side of her that likes boasting about sadism, and evoke her as a kind of best friend, a gal pal, a cross between a girl guide and a fairy godmother. Their evasion admits that Madonna plugs into men's fear and loathing when she flaunts the insatiable pussy.

The mythology of ungovernable female appetite can't be made to work for women; ironies, subversion, inversion, pastiche, masquerade, appropriation—these postmodern strategies all buckle in the last resort under the weight of culpability the myth has entrenched. It permeates the furious response, for instance, to the increasing numbers of single mothers. Instead of inquiring into the causes of marriage breakdown, into the background to so many fatherless families, into the reasons women have become heads of households, instead of attending to the needs of women who are raising children on their own, instead of acknowledging the responsibility most of them are showing towards the task of mothering, and recognising the way the work of care still stitches together the torn fabric of society, lone mothers have come under prolonged and continuing attack. Newspapers, television programs, the conservative cabinet, let fly with one accusation after another; one scare story after another: Home alone children of single, working mothers, home alone children of lesbian couples, opportunistic teenage deviants, and welfare swindlers or at least leeches, spawning child murderers, breeding monsters.

Young criminals—themselves demonised—flourish at the hands of the lone mother, especially, we are told, if she isn't a widow, or an abandoned woman, but unmarried. And the authorities respond: a prison sentence is handed down for a woman who left her child at home when she went to work—as if sending the mother to jail would give the child the help she needed. The recent budget allowing the vital principle that a mother cannot work without some arrangement of child care was at last a step in the right direction.

But the same policy makers who deregulate, who throw employment and housing onto the mercy of market forces, want to regulate the family. It would be better if they stopped their law-and-order ranting and looked clearly at the social revolution that is taking place: in the UK alone, sixty-five per cent of single parents were once married to the fathers of the children. But they are now coping on their own, in almost one in five families in this country; three out of four of these heads of households are women. Like the heir to the throne, more than one in six of his future subjects are being raised by their mothers on their own: they are however rather less well off, as these families are amongst the poorest in the country. One of the reasons the public isn't specially afraid that Prince William will turn out a hooligan but will most likely thrive has more to do with the comforts he enjoys than the state of his parents' marriage.

Women are for the most part doing the best they can in the

circumstances—and learning to survive as they go. Sometimes this entails choosing to keep the family away from the father. Very few of the families have actively sought the circumstances in which they find themselves; in some cases, when the women claim with pride they have indeed chosen, it is worth recalling, without condescension, that if the man in question could or did behave differently, they might think otherwise. And the new self-esteem they can assert is extremely valuable, indeed vital, to their children's own sense of worth. This is the one aspect of feminism that has brushed some of these mothers.

What no thundering moralist has yet seen is that among the young, unmarried mothers whom they are most angry about many have actually gone 'back to basics': they're fulfilling the most ingrained conservative view of woman's function. They are carrying on the make-believe games encouraged by girls' toys— one of the current selling lines is a set of quintuplets, five babies equipped with five sets of nappies, five strollers, five cradles, and so forth. Having and looking after children gives women a recognised part to play; they have this social function—and they have it over men.

Yet the bitter, angry, ignorant view persists, that we inhabit an imaginary cosmos where women on top are somehow killing men and usurping Daddy's throne, where Madonna gyrates and strips to proclaim she's in control, that women are spearheading some feminist revolution, having it all their own way because they've been allowed to slip all traditional moral restraints.

I'm not saying that exploitations and abuses don't happen. Nor am I denying that some women are having babies on their own on purpose. Nor am I ignoring the difference between young women's sense of a role, and many young men's sense of being adrift, with no mooring in sight. But chronic scare-mongering about female behaviour—about wild sexuality and aberrant maternity—distorts understanding and sinks matters of urgent social policy—the proper provision of child care, tax reform, job training and retraining, nursery schools, housing, play areas—into a quagmire of prejudice.

A myth is a kind of story told in public, which people tell one another; they wear an air of ancient wisdom, but that is part of their seductive charm. Not all antiques are better than a modern design—especially if they're needed in ordinary, daily use. But myth's own secret cunning means that it pretends to present the matter as it is and always must be, at its heart lies the principle, in the famous formula of Roland Barthes, that history is turned into nature. But, contrary to this understanding, myths aren't writ in stone, they're not fixed, but often, telling the story of the same figures—of Medea or of dinosaurs—change dramatically both in content and meaning. Myths offer a lens which can be used to see human identity in its social and cultural context—they can lock us up in stock reactions, bigotry and fear, but they're not immutable, and by unpicking them, the stories can lead to others. Myths convey values and expectations which are always evolving, in the process of being formed, but—and this is fortunate—never set so hard they cannot be changed again, and newly told stories can be more helpful than repeating old ones. Both Freud and Jung adapted the long classical tradition of allegorical interpretations, reading the mythical corpus of narratives, learned and popular, in order to unlock symbolic, psychic explanations of human consciousness and behaviour. The paradoxical rationality of myth, the potential of figments to disclose the truth about ourselves, has become the fruitful premise of much contemporary thinking about the mind and personality; the enlightenment distinction between logic and fantasy has given way in the growing realisation that the structures of the imagination, often highly ordered and internally consistent, themselves form understanding. Pleas for a return to reason, for simply stripping away illusion, ignore the necessity and the vitality of mythical material in consciousness as well as unconsciousness.

There's a beauty and the beast story that I'd like to tell you, because like many fairy tales, it shows that things are never quite as they seem and that surprises can spring from any quarter. 'The Wedding of Sir Gawain and Dame Ragnell' is a verse romance written in the mid-fifteenth century by a forgotten and nameless English poet. It reworks the familiar fairy-tale theme of a young man's union with a she-monster, and by the way produces a happy story, at first bawdy, later tender, about the possibility of mutual love and trust, against the odds.

King Arthur, out hunting one day, falls foul of a terrible warlock, who agrees to spare him only on condition that he discovers, within a year, the answer to that fundamental question: What do women want? If King Arthur cannot give the right answer, his head is forfeit. When his time of grace is almost up, Arthur comes across a terrible hag, a lady so foul the poet lets rip with a full-blown comic lexicon of loathliness. She knows the true answer, and she'll pass it on to Arthur, but only if he gives her Sir Gawain for a husband. This is a bitter blow; however, when Arthur tells Gawain, Gawain, that pattern of chivalry, wants nothing better than to serve his liege lord, and agrees to the match. The loathly lady then reveals:

We desire of men above all manner of things
To have the sovereignty . . .

Of all, both high and low.
For where we have sovereignty all is ours
Though a knight be never so fierce,
And ever the mastery win . . .
Of the most manliest is our desire:
To have the sovereignty of such a sire;
Such is our craft and gin

So to the question what do women want—which would vex Freud so deeply later—the answer is sovereignty. And womanly wiles—women's craft and gins—tend to this hidden purpose. This solution, spoken to a classical or a Christian audience, where the subordination of women was considered nature or-dained by divine commandment, automatically conjures the sex-ual and political nightmare of rule by women—velociraptors doing just as they please.

But the tale of the loathly lady subsequently takes a surprising turn against the grain of its own misogyny. For after Arthur's correct answer redeems him from the warlock's clutches, Gawain does indeed marry the foul hag, Dame Ragnell, with her boar's tusk teeth and hanging paps, and in bed on the wedding night, gallantly consents to kiss her. Whereupon, he finds he holds in his arms: 'the fairest creature/That ever he saw . . .'

She tells him she's bound by a spell, and then puts an old, fey riddle to Gawain: would he have her fair by night and foul by day, or vice versa? It is to this conundrum that the perfect knight answers: 'Do as ye list now, my lady gay'.

By allowing her sovereignty at that moment, Gawain performs the final magic which undoes the spell, and his loathly lady's transformed, becoming fair both by day and night. And they live together in great happiness—but for only five years, for then, the poet tells us in a line which pulls the romance oddly into history, she tragically dies young.

The story, based on the same material Chaucer used for the Wife of Bath in *The Canterbury Tales,* can be read at one level as yet another medieval joke about wilful wives, henpecked husbands, as a hostile parable about women on top—or it can be taken to point towards a utopian destination—of negotiated exchanges, of generosity and trust. Sovereignty here can of course be interpreted as domination, and the legend as a burlesque commentary on women's lusts—for sex and mastery—a cautionary tale about the secret will to power of all women which men must recognise and control. But the story's sudden swerve out of comedy into romance, out of bawdy into lyricism, promises high rewards for mutual respect, and extols Gawain for his courtesy towards the loathsome, despised old hag. Sovereignty over self—not over others; the right to govern one's own person, not the right to govern others. The loathly lady gives him love, Gawain brings about her restored shape, her emancipation through his growing understanding.

As a footnote to this look at the serpentine metamorphoses of the monstrous female, I'd like to direct your notice to some scientific data about the praying mantis:

Eckehard Liske and W. Jackson Davis of Santa Cruz, California . . . videotaped the mantises' courtship while the insects thought they were in private and found a pleasant ritual dance in place of cannibalism—and with both partners surviving. The researchers say that until now scientists have distracted the insects by their presence and by watching them under bright lights—and that they didn't give them enough to eat.

This most loved creature in the surrealist bestiary of misogynist folklore, this insect famous for devouring her mate alive after mating, has been vindicated. Let them alone, give them enough to eat and look! they fall into peaceful mutual post-coital slumber.

TWO

BOYS WILL BE BOYS

The Making of the Male

As I was going to the Future Entertainment Show, held in Olympia last year, I soon found I was the only woman waiting for the tube. The station was unusually full for the middle of the morning, with scattered young men in jeans and sneakers, gaggles of young boys, one or two fathers. When the train came and the carriage doors opened, a rather dazed-looking London pigeon fluttered out. A man near me laughed, 'Don't worry,' he said, 'it's only a virtual reality pigeon.'

I streamed into the show with the crowd, clutching my razzle-dazzle, high-tech, impossible-to-forge ticket, and plunged into the roaring hall. The video games industry has grown in value from almost nothing to $1 billion over the last four years. On multiple screens the season's new offerings in interactive play and 3D simulation were being triggered by the very latest in ergonomic joypads to keep bleeping, scrolling, beaming up, blasting, crashing, bursting into flames and starting up again. I wasn't the only woman any longer: there were one or two grannies, one or two mums. And the marketing staff on the stalls were almost all women—'skirt power' to the trade—and they were selling and busking in green bug costumes as Zools or Zoozes or other technical gremlins. But we were interlopers. It was a man's world: the customers and players were almost all boys.

In the 'chill out zone' in the gallery, at stands and on platforms, the players at the banked consoles of games were busy zapping and slicing and chopping and headbutting and dragon punching. Popular culture teems with monsters, with robots, cyborgs and aliens, fiends, mutants, vampires and replicants. Millennial turmoil, the disintegration of so many familiar political blocs and the appearance of new national borders, ferocious civil wars, global catastrophes from famine to AIDS, threats of ecological disasters—of another Chernobyl, of larger holes in the ozone—all these dangers feed fantasies of the monstrous. At the same time, scientific achievements in genetics, reproduction, cosmetic surgery, and transplants have also raised tough and unresolved ethical anxieties about the manufacture of new beings. These are reflected in myths at every level of our culture: in the plots of books, in films, advertisements, song lyrics—and games.

Film's realism, enhanced by the whole revolutionary gamut of illusory techniques, from camera-shot live animation to computer-generated texture mapping, places phantoms within grasp of the sensations. These monsters are made actual, they seem to surround us. The manuals accompanying the role-playing game of 'Dungeons and Dragons' illustrate the Ghast or the Ghoul, the Flail Snail or the Dimensional Shambler with diagrams of their thumb-grip and their bite, and provide maps of where they roam. And in games like 'Streets of Rage', 'Mortal Kombat', 'Instruments of Chaos', 'Night Trap', 'Cannon Fodder', 'Street Fighter', 'Legacy of Sorasil', 'The Rise of the Robots', 'Zombie Apocalypse', 'Psycho Santa', 'Splatterhouse'—the hero slays monsters. Just as Jason and his Argonauts did or Hercules and his Twelve Labours—indeed some of the games quote classical adventures and their pantheons.

Sometimes rescuing a maiden offers a pretext for the exploits, sometimes control or domination of the imaginary horror leads to treasure, as it did to the Golden Fleece or to the Golden Apple of the Hesperides. But the computer's capacity to proliferate means that in video games there be many many dragons, many monsters, many enemies, many aliens, one after another, and they have to be shot'n'blasted, hacked'n'slashed, one by one, level by level as the player works through the stacked platforms of the plot. Some maze puzzles, some role-playing games require strategy, but mostly, the hero busts his way through. A review described 'Rivet', a contest between Robocop and Terminator: 'It's total cyberpunk ultraviolence. The kind of game where you just kill everything. It's great.' The treasure and the wisdom attained at the end of the slaughter—the pause before it begins again—confer authority, in other words, power.

Myths and monsters have been interspliced since the earliest extant poetry from Sumer: the one often features the other. The word 'myth', from the Greek, means a form of speech, while the word 'monster' is derived, in the opinion of one Latin grammarian, from *monstrum*, via *moneo*, and encloses the notions of advising, of reminding, above all of warning. But *moneo*, in the word *monstrum*, has come under the influence of Latin *monstrare*, to show, and the combination neatly characterises the form of speech myth often takes: a myth shows something, it's a story spoken to a purpose, it issues a warning, it gives an account which advises and tells often by bringing into play showings of fantastical shape and invention—monsters. Myths define enemies and aliens and in conjuring them up they say who we are and what we want, they tell stories to impose structure and order. Like fiction, they can tell the truth even while they're making it all up.

The appearance of monsters is intrinsic to at least one kind of fundamental mythological story—the story of origins. Dragons, serpents and beasts multiply in the genealogies of the gods and the origins of the created world. Even the Bible's monotheism allows a glimpse or two of Leviathan and Behemoth—dragons lingering on from the cosmologies of the Babylonians and Assyrians. The presence of monsters also marks the beginning of nations, of cities—think of St George and the Dragon, and of Cadmus who sowed the Dragon's teeth to build and people Thebes. In Antwerp, in the sixteenth century, the city fathers were still showing distinguished visitors the bones of Druon Antigoon, the giant who had been slain by the first king of the region, Brabo, friend and relation of Julius Caesar. The gargantuan shoulder blade and magnificent rib actually belonged to a sperm whale, but they served very well to represent the vanquishing of the brute—and the coming of civilisation to Antwerp.

Chaos threatens in various forms: the she-monster Chimaera spat fire from three heads but the hero Bellerophon, flying down on the winged horse Pegasus, pierced her in her fiery gullet— the flames melted his speartip and she choked to death as the lead cooled inside her. Chimaera's name came to mean illusion: the ultimate monster of monsters, who is both frighteningly there and yet a spectre, who shows something real that at the same time only exists in the mind.

Reason can be awake and beget monsters. Extreme, fantastical, and insubstantial as they are, they materialise real desires and fears, they embody meaning at a deep, psychic level. We're living in a new age of faith of sorts, of myth-making, of monsters, of chimaeras. And these chimaeras define human identity—especially the role of men.

In Mary Shelley's novel, *Frankenstein,* published in 1818, one of the dominant myths today finds its most powerful and tragic expression; the book's central figures have leaped the boundaries of the novel itself into all kinds of retellings, parodic and straight—it's no accident that it's being remade yet again for the screen this year with Kenneth Branagh and Robert de Niro. *Frankenstein* has become *the* contemporary parable of perverted science, but this reading overlooks the author's much more urgent message. Mary Shelley grasped the likelihood that a man might make a monster in his own image and then prove incapable of taking responsibility for him. When the creature at last confronts Victor Frankenstein, the creator who shuns him, he pleads with him, using 'thou', the archaic address of intimacy:

'I am thy creature, and I will be even mild and docile to my natural lord and king if thou wilt also perform thy part, the which thou owest me. Oh, Frankenstein, be not equitable to every other and trample upon me alone, to whom thy justice, and even thy clemency and affection, is most due. Remember that I am thy creature; I ought to be thy Adam, but I am rather the fallen angel, whom thou drivest from joy for no misdeed. Everywhere I see bliss, from which

I alone am irrevocably excluded. I was benevolent and good; misery made me a fiend. Make me happy and I shall again be virtuous.'

'Begone! I will not hear you. There can be no community between you and me; we are enemies. Begone, or let us try our strength in a fight, in which one must fall.'

Victor Frankenstein rejects and wants to destroy the being he's generated from his own intelligence and imagination; he can only flee, and then, when confronted, offer mortal combat—in the desire to be the victor, as his name suggests. The book *Frankenstein* offers a dazzling allegory of monsters' double presence: at one level they're emanations of ourselves, but at another, they're perceived as alien, abominable and separate so that we can deny them, and zap them into oblivion at the touch of a button.

But monsters in the new, nightmare pandemonium of popular culture have something in common which distinguishes them in a crucial way from the ancient Hydra or Medusa or Chimaera: they don't emanate from nature, but they're either men—or man-made. Frankenstein's creature is their immediate ancestor in this too—but Shelley doesn't set up a superior warrior figure to vanquish her monster; her novel pleads on the creature's behalf: he's capable of goodness if Frankenstein would only love him and teach him and include him, not abandon him to his pariah state. The remedy for Frankenstein's hubris doesn't lie in destroying the monster; Shelley writes explicitly against dealing with evil by heroic, lethal exploits. Implicitly, she's recasting the monstrous in the image of its creator: the creature issues from Frankenstein as his brainchild who's also his double, who acts to define him. Here, the beast is the one who knows this, and presses his maker to accept it. Frankenstein's instant, murderous hostility to his creation may resonate with some of Mary Shelley's own disillusion with her father and her husband and their revolutionary ambitions. It may reflect her feelings about male and female antagonism. But its mainspring is located in her hero's self-loathing: her extraordinary and brilliant book inaugurates a new breed of monster, one who isn't ultimately alien, but my brother, my self.

When popular myth places characters like Slugathon or Robocop centre stage, and then annihilates them until the next avatar appears, they're conjuring the perverted products of human intelligence. Unlike Mary Shelley's book, these plotlines almost invariably reject the offspring of science and propose the enemy monster's defeat through force. Nobody in this kind of story sits down to learn to talk, as Frankenstein's creature does so poignantly and so elaborately when he eavesdrops on the English lessons given in the woodland cottage by the old man and his family to the beautiful Arabian fugitive, Safie. Current tales of conflict and extermination never hear the monster say: 'I am malicious, because I am miserable.' Or, 'Make me happy, and I shall again be virtuous.' The phrases sound absurd, because we're so accustomed to expect the hero to have no other way of managing the monsters than slaying them.

Monsters who manifest their nature, like Frankenstein's creature, clearly present easier targets than those in disguise. Deception is a theme that runs through the history of fantasy art, which itself constitutes an attempt to deceive. It achieves a brilliant apotheosis with the replicants of *Blade Runner*, Ridley Scott's cult movie. Replicants are androids, impervious, almost invulnerable; but they look like humans and have been artificially provided with memories of childhood and they don't know that they're monsters. As the word android implies, they're men—

and yet not men at the same time. Philip K. Dick's book, on which *Blade Runner* is based, puts the dilemma succinctly in its witty title, *Do Androids Dream of Electric Sheep?* This is the ultimate, representative nightmare of this fin de siècle. A hundred and fifty odd years ago, Frankenstien's creature suffered because he knew his own deformity. Jekyll and Hyde knew each other well, though the evil Hyde, as his name tells us, was already concealed within Jekyll. This is still optimistic stuff compared to *Blade Runner*. The film—and the book—touch a live contemporary nerve when they imagine that the robotic monsters look just like humans, that their nature isn't apparent—neither to us, nor to them.

The acute, painful problem today is that these manufactured monsters are ourselves; and ourselves especially as the male of the species. A recent shift in the telling of an old, widely distributed legend illustrates rather well the new fascination and unease surrounding men: in this urban myth, a woman living alone hears a strange sound coming from her kitchen, and going in, sees a hand working its way through an opening that's just been sawn in the door. So she takes a poker, lays it in the fire and when it's glowing attacks the hand, which instantly withdraws, with a howl of pain.

The next day, the woman bumps into the child who lives next door, who tells her by the way that her father has gone to hospital—with a terrible burn on his hand.

In the old, familiar version, the intruder was a witch, a recurrent monster in such creepy tales; but she's turned into a man—an ordinary family man, a neighbour who—and this is crucial—doesn't *look* dangerous.

Fear of men has grown alongside belief that aggression—including sexual violence—inevitably defines the character of the young male. Another myth shadows the contemporary concept of male nature: that intruder could be a rapist. Alongside the warrior, the figure of the sex criminal has dug deep roots in the cultural formation of masculinity. The kids who kill a series of ghouls or aliens can tell themselves they are not like the monsters they are killing. But the serial killer—the very term is of recent coinage—has a human face like theirs. He's dominated contemporary folklore, a figure of thrill and dread, for a hundred years. The terror of Jack the Ripper gripped the Victorians, and present-day murderers are now interviewed on television from prison. The part work magazine, *Real-Life Crimes,* giving details and methods, sells around 60,000 copies an issue.

Films—and the books they're based on—often mete out punishment to sexual women, in the same way as spectators of the Ripper's victims in the London Dungeon enjoy the horror even as they shudder at it. But video games are more scrupulous about current taboos: most of their heroes can't be seen to attack and murder women as such—with the result that women have pretty much disappeared from the plots altogether. There's the occasional dewy-eyed girl hoodlum or pixie-haired hellraiser or 'salacious spider woman' and there are some female streetfighters—all active, assertive types and good examples of how positive imaging can backfire. And, as I said, the stock motive of the damsel in distress recurs. But the effect of the almost total absence of women from this all-engulfing imaginary world of boys is to intensify the sense of apartness, of alienation, of the deep oppositeness of the female sex.

Modern myths still approach the enigma of sexual difference using very old simple formulae—and if the girls are getting tough, the tough get tougher. In this emphasis on warrior strength, the new stories conform to very ancient ones, stories which were grounded in the different social circumstances of a military or pastoral, archaic society—the heroes of Greece, the samurai of Japan. Slaying monsters, controlling women, still offers a warrant for the emerging hero's heroic character; this feeds the definition of him as a man. But this narrative is so threadbare, it has come away from the studs that held it to the inner stuff of experience: warrior fantasies today offer a quick rush of compensatory power, but pass on no survival skills—either for a working or a family life.

When the young Achilles is hidden by his mother in women's clothes, because she knows from an oracle that he's to die in the Trojan War, it proves child's play to winkle him out. Odysseus the crafty one disguises himself as a merchant and goes to the court of Lycomedes, among whose daughters Achilles has been concealed. Odysseus devises a kind of Trojan Horse: a chestful of gifts, overflowing with jewels and trinkets and textiles—and precious weapons.

The king's daughters bedeck themselves, of course, but Achilles girds himself over his frock with sword and buckler and is unmasked by a triumphant Odysseus and carried off to win the war for the Greeks. Piquant baroque paintings also exist of the warrior revealed, grasping his weapon while the girls primp, and the subject inspired a baroque tragicomic opera by Metastasio, as well as a broader English version, called *Achilles in Petticoats*.

But the mighty Greek heroes aren't the only models of the male. Achilles might choose a mighty sword and buckler, and Hercules use muscle power and a big stick, but in the fairy-tale tradition, by contrast, heroes develop other skills. In *The Arabian Nights* a poor fisherman finds a bottle in his nets, and when he opens it, a huge angry ogre of a genie rises up and threatens the fisherman with instant death. The fisherman responds that he can't believe that anyone so awesome and so magnificent could ever have fitted into such a little bottle—and begs the genie to show him how he did it. The genie obliges, and gradually winds himself into the vessel. The fisherman jumps on it, stoppers it up in a trice. He then refuses to let the genie out until he's granted him fabulous riches.

'Cunning and high spirits' are the mark of those hopeful myths which imagine a different world, which hold out a promise of happiness—and transformation. The story ends, 'The fisherman became the richest man of his day, and his daughters were the wives of kings till the end of their lives.' Some sceptics might object that the cunning hero or the lucky simpleton doesn't belong in epic or tragedy, where the ideals of manliness are forged; but fairy-tale elements are impossible to keep separate from the grandest of myths: when Oedipus, too, meets the Sphinx, it's a battle of wits. No bloodshed accompanies his defeat of her reign of terror—after solving her riddle, he just leaves her, whereupon, her mystery undone, she hurls herself from a precipice.

In Homer, Odysseus tells the Cyclops that his name is Nobody. So, when Odysseus blinds the Cyclops in his one eye, the giant howls for help to his father the god of the sea and the other Olympians. But all the gods hear is his cry, 'Nobody has blinded me.' And so they do nothing.

This trick from the *Odyssey* is literally one of the oldest in the book. The hero who lives by his wits survives in countless hard-luck, Puss in Boots–style stories. The prankster or riddler who—fool though he might be—makes good against the odds, flourishes in the folklore of people all over the world; he travelled from West Africa to the Caribbean, for example, in the figure of Anansi, the spider, and features in the stories told there since the seventeenth century.

Charlie Chaplin, and even Woody Allen, have worked this groove, the heroic pathetic. But a gleeful use of cunning and high spirits against brute force, a reliance on subterfuge have almost faded from heroic myth today. In the prevailing popular concept of masculinity, as reflected in comics, rock bands, street fashion, Clint Eastwood or Arnold Schwarzenegger movies, the little man, the riddler or trickster, has yielded before the type of warrior hero, the paradigm of the fittest survivor.

It's striking to see, from old footage of the Olympic Games, how skinny and scrawny athletes used to be: the bigness of men—body-building, muscle-toning—has never been so important to gender definition as it is today.

This contemporary belief that fitness is literally embodied in physical size neglects to pay attention to the rather more important question: what kind of way of life are the survivors defending, what society are they making? It's interesting that the doctrine of the survival of the fittest has become conventional wisdom—opposing theories have pointed out that the animal cooperation and respect for resources are rather more necessary for survival than dog eats dog. But ideas which stress thoughtful and mutual divisions and exchanges in nature sound like marginal, utopian, New Age crankery. Cunning intelligence—in Greek, the goddess Metis—has been superseded by force as the wellspring of male authority, of power; in today's morality, force even feels somehow cleaner, purer, more upright. The very word 'wily', the very idea of subterfuge, carry a stain of dishonour. Boys are not raised to be cozeners or tricksters—it'd be unthinkable to train the future man in lures and wiles and masks and tricks; they're brought up to play with Action Man, and his heavy-duty, futuristic Star Wars arsenal; they're taught to identify with Ninja Turtles, as crusaders, vigilantes, warriors on behalf of the planet, to flick a transformer toy from a flash car into a heavy-duty fighting exoskeleton, bristling with weapons, a monster of technological innovation—the Terminator, Robocop. There are even games with a create-your-own-deity option, in which, having chosen 'which god you want to be', you then acquire nearly thirty ways 'of smiting your enemy'. The army recognises the link between such narratives and their recruitment needs: they take prominent advertisements in the specialist advanced computer games magazines.

I'm not advancing the con man over the soldier, or the cozener over the honest gentleman—that would be absurd; I'm observing a trend towards defining male identity and gender through visible, physical, sexualised signs of potency rather than verbal, mental agility.

Such signs course through the hardening capillaries of the social system with unprecedented fluidity, carried by a thousand different conduits in a million images and sound bites. It's so obvious, but it bears repeating: no participant in the mysteries celebrating the exploits of Hercules, no member of the audience at the tragedy of Agamemnon or Jason had the story recapitulated and reproduced and beamed at him—or her—again and again in a frenzied proliferation of echoes. This use of repetition combines with another new and very popular form of storytelling: the advertisement. The principal task of an ad—to persuade—has altered response to the myths advertising often absorbs and reinterprets. Sometimes ads do give warnings—as in public safety campaigns. But these are recognised to be ambiguous, and warnings against drugs can be taken all too easily as glamorising invitations to sample them. Almost always, ads trigger desire and excite imitation and identification.

The mythic heroes of the Greek story cycles, like Oedipus, like Jason, like Orestes, served as tragic warnings; their pride, their knowing and unknowing crimes, the matricides and infanticides, self-blindings and suicides, all the strife and horror they undergo and perpetrate didn't make them exemplary, but cautionary: they provoked terror and pity, not emulation. The tragedies they inspired offered their heroes as objects of debate, not models. No one coming out of *Oedipus at Colonus* would feel he wanted to be Oedipus in the way that a spaghetti Western excites hero-worship for Clint Eastwood.

But in the arenas of contemporary culture—the TV channel, the computer game, the toy shop, the street—traditional mythic figures of masculinity like the warrior and the rapist circulate and recirculate every day, setting up models, not counterexamples, and the forms which convey them do not contain argument or counter-argument, as in a Greek tragedy, but reiterate the message, as in an advertisement. They're appealing to the group's purchasing power, shaping tastes, playing on rivalry and vulnerability. They don't cry, 'Beware', but rather 'Aspire!'

Boys will be boys, people say when they mean aggression, violence, noise, guns. But does the warrior ethic, which exposed Achilles in the women's quarters, fit the needs of our civil society? Why does an age which believes in medical and scientific intervention on a heroic scale, which works for change—and delivers it—coexist with a determinist philosophy about human nature and gender? The point about Frankenstein assembling the monster from body parts haunts contemporary consciousness, but the book's main philosophical argument, that his viciousness is learned, not innate, is somehow overlooked. The biological and genetic revolution already upon us can alter and save bodies, but stories which feature such bodies assume that their natures are static, determined, doomed—rare is the character in a video game or comic strip who develops or learns to be different. Yet anthropology has shown that, in the territory of sexuality as well as other human areas, social expectation affects character. Masculinity varies from group to group, place to place, and its varieties are inculcated, not naturally so.

Societies who expect boys to be unflinching warriors subject them to rituals of traumatic severity in order to harden them. Among the Sambia in New Guinea, a tribe in which men are warriors and hunters and women are feared and despised, boys are removed into exclusive male control around the age of six, and begin a series of violent initiations which will turn them into men like their fathers. Proper, cultural masculinity doesn't come naturally, it seems, to a New Guinea Highlander. Why should it to a child living in Kentish Town or Aberdeen?

Among other, rather less remote people, living today in the Balkans, in the mountains of Montenegro, the birth of a daughter inspires routine, ritual lamentation. Blood feuds are handed down from generation to generation, and if there's no son surviving in a family to carry on the feud, a daughter can be raised in his place and become a 'sworn virgin', a warrior in disguise to defend her family like a man. Her true sex will never again, on pain of death, be alluded to either in her presence or out of it.

When the Serbian-Montenegrin forces in the current war in the Balkans cursed the women they raped that they would bear children who would forever be their enemies and fight against their mother and her people, they were behaving according to a particular complex of inherited social beliefs, they were speaking out of commitment to military values, paternal lineage and a cult of male heroism.

I'm not offering an excuse, a rationale, or adequate explanation of men's capacity to rape and kill. But I am rejecting the universalising argument about male nature that the rapes committed in former Yugoslavia are committed simply because men are rapists. This argument goes, in the words of one prominent American rights lawyer, Catharine MacKinnon: 'men do in war what they do in peace, only more so' and also that 'similar acts are common everywhere in peacetime and are widely understood as sex'. These sweeping assertions work against mobilising change; they present as sovereign truth beyond history, beyond society, the idea that the swagger and the cudgel come naturally to men, due to their testosterone, a hormone that according to this view, is always in excess. The Serbian rapist becomes the summation of male nature.

The problem, how to make a man of men without turning out killers and rapists, has inspired a men's movement in America, which is enjoying a huge international success, led by its guru, the poet Robert Bly, and his personal growth best-seller, *Iron John*. Bly rightly notices that women are unhappy about men, that this does not make men happy either, and that the absence of fathers is keenly mourned. Feminism has taught women vibrancy and knowledge, he argues, masculinism must follow its example. Bly advocates the appointment of surrogate fathers—men who take younger men under their protection, and writes admiringly of tribal rites of passage in which men are socialised in this way, alluding to shared blood-letting among the Kikuyu, and other symbolic woundings (so called—the wounds are real enough). Though Bly doesn't actually argue for direct bodily assault, the men's movement has adapted many of the socialising methods used by warrior tribes like the New Guinea Sambia, such as separation from women in male bonding weekends and homoerotic physical contact—though so far none of the men's groups have started practising ritual fellatio of men by boys, as do the Sambia in order to transmit the necessary semen for manhood from generation to generation.

Bullying a boy to become one of the boys has taken physical form, in places rather closer than New Guinea. Today, in the hazings, or initiations practised among college fraternities in America, the idea of entering into a bond with other men also requires submission to secret, physical rituals. The popularity of horror, of blood'n'guts stories, arises from a similar urge to test oneself to the limits: the pleasure may lie in surviving the ordeal. Certainly ads for games like to make jokes about players shitting on themselves: for example, a row of men's briefs on the washing line, and the message, Nincontinent, Nintimidating, Nintendo.

It seems to me that Bly has framed his cure the wrong way round: the monsters of machismo are created in societies where men and women are already too far separated by sexual fear and loathing, segregated by contempt for the prescribed domestic realm of the female, and above all by exaggerated insistence on aggression as the defining characteristic of heroism and power.

The presence of fathers will only reduce the threatening character of maleness flourishing around us if sexual polarities are lessened, not increased. Delinquency among young men has provoked acute alarm recently—one man in three in Britain will have been convicted of a crime by the age of 30. And it's carelessly repeated that single mothers are specially to blame.

But it's interesting to look at the problem of fatherless boys from another angle. The popular argument goes that boys brought up by their mothers alone compensate through violence for the lack of a strong male role model in their lives, that they express the anger they feel at the sole female authority at home. This could be put the other way round: the culture that produces irresponsible fathers openly extols a form of masculinity that is opposed to continuity, care, negotiation, and even cunning—qualities necessary to make lasting attachments between men and children, men and women.

These boys aren't deprived of strong masculine role models, they aren't in rebellion, but are suffering from the compulsion of conforming. They're exposed to blanket saturation in a myth of masterful, individualist independence; they're bit players training to be heroes in a narrative which can proceed only by conflict to rupture. Men have been abandoning their families, and almost half never see their children again after two years.

In Mary Shelley's later, apocalyptic novel, significantly called *The Last Man,* the hero exclaims, ' "This, I thought, is Power! Not to be strong of limb, hard of heart, ferocious and daring; but kind, compassionate and soft." '

It's a measure of the depths of our present failure of nerve that these words sound ridiculous, embarrassing, inappropriate, that Verney's cry strikes one as a heap of hooey—a foolish dream, a chimaera. Mary Shelley's utopianism is too ardent for our cynical times. But we can take away from her work the crucial knowledge that monsters are made, not given. And if monsters are made, not given, they can be unmade, too.

THREE

LITTLE ANGELS,
LITTLE MONSTERS

Keeping Childhood Innocent

In 1828, a young man was found in the market square of Nuremberg; he could write his name, Caspar Hauser, but he couldn't speak, except for a single sentence, 'I want to be a rider like my father.' He had been kept all his life in a cellar alone in the dark until his unexplained release that day. Though he was in his teens when he suddenly appeared, he seemed a symbolic child, a stranger to society, a *tabula rasa* in whom ignorance and innocence perfectly coincided. In his wild state, Caspar Hauser offered his new minders and teachers a blueprint of human nature—untouched. And in his case, his character fulfilled the most idealised image of original innocence.

He was sick when given meat to eat, passed out when given beer, and showed so little aggression and cruelty that he picked off his fleas without crushing them to set them free through the bars of his cell. His story attracted myth-making in his own time, and has continued to inspire writers and filmmakers. The most recent work, a book-length narrative poem by David Constantine, opens with the apparition of Caspar Hauser out of nowhere:

He stood there swaying on his sticky feet,

His head was bowed, the light hurt his eyes,
The pigeons ran between his feet like toys
And he was mithered by the scissoring swifts . . .
Even an embryo
Raises its little paws against the din
But Caspar stood there sucking it all in

Dowsing for more of it on the square's navel,
Arms stiff like compasses, at the end of one
He held his letter of introduction

'To whom it may concern' and at the end
Of the other a wide-awake hat,
Both very tightly. There he remained . . .

until the windows
Folded their wooden lids back and in rows . . .

From all the openings of their ordinary lives
The people stared . . .

They inched, already aghast
At all the questions he would make them ask.

Caspar Hauser was an enigma, and after his mysterious return to the world, his life was never free from strange, turbulent incident: he was suspected of fabrication, he was assaulted and wounded by an unknown assailant, and later, was thought to be the usurped heir to the throne of Baden. His innate gentle goodness couldn't save him: he was attacked, seduced, betrayed, and abandoned by his would-be adoptive father, the Englishman Lord Stanhope. And finally he was murdered, in still unsolved circumstances, in 1833.

There'd been other wild children who'd inspired scientific experiments into human development, but Caspar Hauser more than any other foreshadows this century's struggle with the question of the child's natural character. And his fate still offers a timely parable about the nostalgic worship of childhood innocence, which is more marked today than it ever has been: the difference of the child from the adult has become a dominant theme in contemporary mythology. In literature this has produced two remarkable dream figures living in voluntary exile from grown-up society—Kipling's unforgettably vivid Mowgli, and J. M. Barrie's cocky hero, the boy who wouldn't grow up, Peter Pan. Both reveal the depth of adult investment in a utopian childhood state. This can lead to disillusion, often punitive and callous, with the young as people. The shock of James Bulger's death was deepened by his murderers' ages, yet their trial revealed a brutal absence of pity for them as children. It was conducted as if they were adults not because they had behaved with adult consciousness, but because they had betrayed an abstract myth about children's proper childlikeness.

The belief that there's a proper childlike way for children to be has deep roots. In his novel about Caspar Hauser written in

1908, the German writer Jacob Wassermann put his finger on the dreams the boy stirred:

> This creature reeling helplessly in an alien world, his gaze cumbered with sleep, his gestures curbed by fear, his noble brow enthroned above a somewhat wasted face, the peace and purity of heart that appear in that brow: to my mind, they are incontestable signs. If my suspicions prove correct, if I can lay bare the roots of this life and make its branches blossom, I shall hold up a mirror of immaculate humanity to our dull insensitive world, and people will see that there are valid proofs of the existence of the soul—which the idolaters of our times deny with so squalid a vehemence.

In this ringing declaration we catch the full expression of a belief which still has purchase today, seventy years on: that the child and the soul are somehow interchangeable, and that consequently children are the keepers and the guarantors of humanity's reputation. This has inspired a wonderfully rich culture of childhood, one of the most remarkable phenomena of modern society—from an unsurpassed imaginative literature for children today to deep psychoanalytical speculation on the thinking processes and even language of the foetus. But it also has social consequences for children themselves that are not all benign.

Childhood, placed at a tangent to adulthood, perceived as special and magical, precious and dangerous at once, has turned into some volatile stuff—hydrogen, or mercury, which has to be contained. The separate condition of the child has never been so bounded by thinking, so established in law as it is today. This mythology is not fallacious, or merely repressive—myths are not only delusions—chimaeras—but also tell stories which can give shape and substance to practical, social measures. How we treat children really tests who we are, fundamentally conveys who we hope to be.

The separate sphere of childhood has grown—as a social concept, as a market possibility, as an area of research, as a problem: children are no longer chattels, any more than women, and new legal measures like the Children's Act give them voice in choices and decision-making about their legal situation. Incest, molestation and even rape in families have always taken place, but never have more attempts been made—often with appalling clumsiness—to save children from their violators.

Fiction and reportage also focus on the child as so radically different that he or she stands in an oblique relation to human society, not entirely part of it, not yet incorporated into history. Charities in hard-pressed competition for funds resort to more and more explicit images of maimed, starving, diseased, orphaned, and doomed infants and children in order to raise money for schemes which are frequently intended to help everyone— like cancer research, water purification. The children in the photographs provide a solution to what could be called 'the Oxfam syndrome': how to portray the need and poverty of others without making it look like their endemic, perennial hopelessness. Images of children, who are vulnerable and dependent in every society, whatever its circumstances, help to evade that implicit condescension.

The injured child has become today's icon of humanity. It's no accident that the Victorian melodrama *Les Misérables* inspired one of the contemporary theatre's greatest successes, that the saucer-eyed, starveling waif staring from the posters drew thousands to the musical. The phantom face of James Bulger has become the most haunting image of present horrors and social failure—his innocence an appeal and an accusation.

Some historians, like Philippe Ariès, have suggested—rather influentially—that the comparative offhandedness towards children in the past denotes indifference and that the kind of love we expect and know today is a comparatively modern phenomenon, a bourgeois luxury. Certainly hardly any examples of children's own writings or paintings survive, and few records of their behaviour have come down, until parents—in seventeenth-century Holland, for instance—began keeping diaries. But this doesn't necessarily mean parents didn't care. The testimony of graves yields another story: from Roman epitaphs to memorials in Westminster Abbey, the accents of grief sound across the centuries. On a tomb in the Etruscan necropolis of Cerveteri, near Rome, a father had these verses written for his daughter Asiatica:

Here lies the lifeless body of my beloved little girl, who has been plunged into a bitter death by the Fates—her unlucky life had lasted less than ten years. Cruel fates, who have saddened my old age! For I shall always seek, little Asiatica, to see your face again, shaping its features in my mind to find some consolation. My only solace will be to see you again, as soon as ever possible, when, my life over, our two shades will be united.

Not only tombs, but stories too convey the intense attachment felt for children. In tragedy, the murders of offspring provide the believable motive for the most terrible revenges: Clytemnestra never forgets that Agamemnon allowed her daughter Iphigenia to be sacrificed to get a fair wind for Troy. For this, in Euripides's play, she makes the first literal bloodbath of him.

It seems to me that children have always been cherished. But the present cult of the child loves them for a new and different reason. It insists on children's intimate connection, above all, to a wonderful, free-floating world of the imagination. Their observable, active fantasy life, their fluid make-believe play seem to give them access to a world of wisdom, and this in turn brings them close to myth and fairy tale. These ideas were grown in the ground of Romanticism: for Wordsworth, heaven lay about us in our infancy and the child was father to the man. He was influenced by the idealism of German metaphysics at the time. The mystical poet Novalis stressed the importance of becoming childlike to gain wisdom: writing about fairy tales, a form he believed held huge possibilities of truth-telling, Novalis noted in his journals, 'A true fairy tale must . . . be a prophetic account of things—an ideal account . . . [the] confessions . . . of an ideal child. A child is a good deal cleverer and wiser than an adult— but the child must be an ironic child.'

Novalis can be heard, in mid-sentence, realising that the claim of childlikeness in a genre like the fairy tale is always ironical— you or I, when we long to be as little children, can only masquerade as such, we can only perform childlikeness as far as we can observe it or recall it. We are doomed to an ironic innocence.

But it is also difficult to grasp how innocence would show itself without adults to influence it—this was the miracle of Caspar Hauser. Novalis's journal entry immediately adds that a child's games are "imitation[s] of grown-ups'. Mummies and Daddies, Doctors and Nurses, Pirates and Soldiers, Cowboys and Indians, Cops and Robbers. How would a child play if there were no grown-ups to imitate? In what games would a child's untouched imagination be different?

The Romantic thirst to recover childlikeness had a huge influence on the growth of interest in children and the activities of their minds. Anthologies with titles like *Myths of the Greeks and Romans; Tanglewood Tales; Tales of the Norse Gods and Heroes,* all treating myth and legend, began to be produced as children's literature in the last century. The childhood of the species—the era of myth and legend—seemed appropriate for the young. And the heroes of wonder narratives of all kinds gradually became younger, to invite the young listener's or reader's identification. This change had certain, serious consequences. The tale of Cupid and Psyche, for instance, which later inspired *Beauty and the Beast,* first appears in the second century, in the ribald, metaphysical novel by Apuleius, *The Golden Ass:* there, it's an adult romance and Cupid and Psyche have been lovers for some time when Psyche breaks the spell by looking at Cupid in bed with her. The Neoplatonists in the Renaissance allegorised the tale as the spiritual quest of the Soul for love—still no hint of child protagonists or a child audience. But by the eighteenth century, the romance itself is transformed into a fairy tale, *Beauty and the Beast.* Filtered through the eyes of a well-meaning governess, it turns into a moral lesson in love, directed at her young charges to prepare them for tricky moments lying ahead: Beauty is certainly not going to bed with the Beast, but deciding whether or not they should get engaged.

At the beginning of the nineteenth century, the Grimm brothers collected the material for their famous collection of German fairy tales. They relied on a heterogeneous group of sources—members of their own family, servants, a tailor's wife, several landed aristocratic friends—all of them adults who had continued to pass on the stories in mixed company of men and women, old and young. The Grimms' full title, *Children's and Household Tales,* retained the hint of a universal audience, but there's no doubt that their pioneering work nourished the concept that such tales belonged in a special way to children. However, the brothers quickly realised that if the tales were to become children's fare, their previous adult entertainment value, their sadism, eroticism, cruelty, and immoral distribution of just and unjust deserts, had to be either censored or explained. This led to clipping and tucking and letting in here and letting out there. On the whole, sex was out and violence was in, and lots of it, especially in the form of gleeful retributive justice. The wicked stepmother in *Snow White* could dance to death in her red-hot shoes, but the Sleeping Beauty—who had borne twins to the prince in earlier versions—could now only be kissed.

The difficulty is that by angling such material at children in particular, the pleasure they took in it marked out bloodthirstiness, fearlessness, and even callousness as childish—rather than universally human—characteristics. By making children the heroes and heroines of such fairy tales, the erotic discoveries and ordeals many of them describe had to be disinfected—leaving sexuality latent in violent symbols and gory plots.

In the postwar period, psychoanalytic thinkers, like Bruno Bettelheim in his influential study *The Uses of Enchantment,* deepened the association of fairy tale with children, and of cruel fantasy with the childish imagination. Bettelheim affirmed the therapeutic value of struggle and horror for the growing child, arguing that as a small, vulnerable creature suffering from adults' tyranny, it was very helpful to read about other small vulnerable creatures, like Cinderella or Tom Thumb, who survived—or better still, won through against all adversity. From this perspective, nothing in fantasy was perceived as too foul or too violent. Brightly coloured picture books of Cinderella now include the bloody chopping of one sister's toes and the lopping of the other's heel, and climax with the putting out of the ugly sisters' eyes.

The theory that children need to compensate for their own hapless dependence by imagining themselves huge and powerful and cruel has also normalised all manner of frightening play-acting, equating children with monsters, childhood with a savage state. Stephen Jay Gould, the biologist, has pointed out that kids don't have an innate kinship with dinosaurs, but that it has been fostered by intensive marketing; the relationship seems based in some idea of shared primitiveness—and future extinction. Lots of toys appeal to the idea of children's savagery: from huge furry, clawed slippers for tiny tots to wear to bed to warn off any other beasts in the night, to dinosaur lunchboxes and watches. As a gift catalogue describes, 'At the touch of a button, the fearsome tyrannosaurus rex emits a blood-curdling little roar.'

In the very midst of consecrating innocence, the modern my-thology of childhood ascribes to children a specially rampant natural appetite for all kinds of transgressive pleasures, including above all the sadomasochistic thrills of fear. And these child heroes—and heroines—now enjoy a monopoly on all kinds of unruly passions which adults later have to learn to control in themselves.

Child protagonists have become so commonplace that the convention has become invisible. In books written for children, from the great Victorian originals, like *The Water Babies* and the two Alice stories, to the Billy Bunter and Angela Brazil series, the Famous Five and the Secret Seven, as well as books by rather more original and inspired contemporaries of ours like Sue Town-send and Joan Aiken, with their vivid protagonists Adrian Mole and Dido Twite, it's become axiomatic that the child reader enjoys identifying with a child. Films reaching—successfully— for the family audience also place children centre stage: in almost all Spielberg vehicles and offshoots, from *E.T.* to *Back to the Future,* children outsmart adults; in *Jurassic Park,* the two kids take the conventional place of the blonde in more adult movies, as victims of the predators on the rampage, until the obligatory ending, when the girl works the computer and saves the day, Enid Blyton—style. Characters like Dorothy in *The Wizard of Oz,* or now Aladdin in the new Disney cartoon, have grown younger and younger as the cinema as a medium grows older.

The tendency isn't limited to the growing market in children's entertainment; the child's-eye view has become one of the most adopted and fertile narrative positions in all media: Henry James explored its dense and poignant ironies in his novel *What Maisie Knew,* still the greatest study of divorce and what the papers call a tug-of-love baby. It's interesting to glance at a list of really successful novels and see just how many adopt a child's eye: from *The Catcher in the Rye* to *Empire of the Sun,* and more recently, Ben Okri's *The Famished Road* and Roddy Doyle's *Paddy Clarke, Ha Ha Ha.* In the cinema, the device gives the camera itself a role: what the child sees, the lens follows, claiming equal im- partiality, of ignorance or innocence. Again, a list includes highly successful films destined for an adult audience: the big-budget *Witness,* the arthouse masterpiece *The Spirit of the Beehive,* or Ingmar Bergman's lyrical and tender memoir, *Fanny and Alex- ander* use the central perspective of a child to draw the spectator into a different angle of vision, to make us accept the camera's pristine truthfulness, to intensify the pathos and the drama. By making us as little children, we are helped to shed cynicism and resistance to the material on view, and to mind more because more is at stake—the image of a child always opens up the horizon to a possible future, and so when the clouds lower, it feels darker.

The nagging, yearning desire to work back to a pristine state of goodness, an Eden of lost innocence, has focussed on children. On the map of contemporary imaginative pathways, J. M. Barrie stands as firmly as the statue of Peter Pan gives West London children their bearings in the park. He truly became a founding father of today's cult of children when in his famous play of 1904, he made the audience responsible for the continued existence of fairyland: the fairy Tinkerbell drinks poison and Peter Pan cries out to the audience, 'Do you believe in fairies? Say quick that you believe! If you believe, clap your hands!' Barry was so anxious that nobody would clap in reply that he paid a claque to do so in the first performances, but then found that it was unnecessary.

Adults applaud their loyalty to the world of pretend and children follow. The statement of faith in fairies signals collusion with Peter Pan, the boy who never grew up—it affirms the connection of the adult with that childhood Eden in which the Lost Boys are still living; it defies the death of the child within. But at this point, a double bind catches us in its toils: for the defiance of itself admits the impossibility of Peter Pan and the Lost Boys' state. Grown-ups want them to stay like that for their sakes, not the children's, and they want children to be simple enough to believe in fairies too, again, for humanity's sake on the whole, to prove something against the evidence.

Contemporary child mythology enshrines children to meet adult desires and dreams, including Romantic and Surrealist yearnings to live through the imagination, with unfettered, unrepressed fantasy; in turn, this presupposes that the child has access to a form of desirable wisdom, of potent innocence which cannot tell pretend from real, and sex from sexlessness, a kind of supernatural irrationality. But perhaps only a Caspar Hauser, raised in total isolation, could ever meet these demands.

The Spielberg school of filmmaking flatters the child audience with a picture of their superiority: not only the computer nerd who saves the show in *Jurassic Park,* but E.T.'s friends, and, above all, the hero of *Back to the Future* who time travels into the past and finds he has to save his own parents there from making a complete mess of their lives. This admiration for children appeals to them, as box office, of course, as all images of heroism do; but it's ambivalent in its effect, since it exaggerates kids' know-how and contributes to the prevailing myth of their apartness, their difference, their unreachability.

Yet, even as I speak, I can hear objections flying thick and fast: for every dozen wonderful innocents in literature or popular culture, there are unsettling figures of youthful untruth and perversity: children today, far from holding up the lit lamp of hope like the little girl in Picasso's 'Guernica', have become the focus of even greater anxiety and horror than their mothers, than even their single mothers. Michael Jackson was once a child performer of exactly that adorable cuddly cuteness that makes grown-ups purr and coo. Now a boy sprite who won't grow up, he epitomises the intense, risky, paradoxical allure of the Peter Pan myth. He leaps and dances and sings 'I'm Bad', gives his estate the name Neverland, draws the passionate worship of millions of children, and then finds himself charged with child abuse.

We call children 'little devils', 'little monsters', 'little beasts'— with the full ambiguous force of the terms, all the complications of love and longing, repulsion and fear. Jesus said 'Suffer the little children to come unto me', and Christianity worships its god as a baby in a manger, but the Christian moral tradition has also held, simultaneously, the inherent sinfulness of children.

Original Sin holds up the spectre of innate human wickedness: whatever glosses theologians put on it, Christian children have been raised to believe that without divine help the species is bound for hell. Grimly, parents and carers confronted child wickedness: in New England, Cotton Mather used to beat his daughter to drive the demons of sin from her, and recommended the practice to his fellow Americans; in 1844, a German pastor wrote the terrifyingly punitive *Struwwelpeter*, with its scissor man and other bogeys for making little boys and girls be good. It's one of the major ironies in the history of children's literature that Heinrich Hoffmann wrote *Struwwelpeter* for his son, to poke fun, Belloc-style, at the moralising tone of current schoolbooks. But the humour of his effort has largely gone missing, and *Struwwelpeter* has joined the shelf of finger-wagging volumes to become one of the nastiest texts ever used to scare the naughtiness out of naughty children.

But the Child has never been seen as such a menacing enemy as today. Never before have children been so saturated with all the power of projected monstrousness to excite repulsion—and even terror. Henry James, in his peculiar, brilliant and troubling ghost story of 1894, *The Turn of the Screw*, defined the unease of the modern dilemma, that even the most beautiful and shining examples may be counterfeit.

When the governess looks at Flora and Miles, she can't conquer her fears that they're indeed possessed by some evil:

To gaze into the depths of blue of the child's eyes and pronounce their loveliness a trick of premature cunning was to be guilty of cynicism in preference to which I naturally preferred to abjure my judgement and, so far as might be, my agitation . . . with our small friends' voices in the air, their pressure on one's heart and their fragrant faces against one's cheek, everything fell to the ground but their incapacity and their beauty . . .

Every knotted phrase of this protestation passes through the teller's continuing, helpless suspicion that the children may look like angels and still be devils underneath.

Today, such doubts match widespread fears, and public grief focusses obsessively on the loss of an ideal of children, of their playfulness, their innocence, their tenderness, their beauty. The child holds up an image of origin, but origins are compounded of good and evil together, battling it out; this conflict spreads rings of disquiet all around. Children are perceived as innocent because they're outside society, pre-historical, pre-social, instinctual, creatures of unreason, primitive, kin to unspoiled nature. Whether this is seen as good or evil often reflects the self-image of the society. Surveillance cameras register the walk of young killers on their way to acts of unimaginable violence; special seats have to be made to raise these child murderers above the level of the dock; my local paper wails, 'Terror Tots Attack Frail Victim'; the most notorious of video nasties is called *Child's Play.*

Bad children—a symptom of modernity—surface again and again in some of the most powerful contemporary fiction, like Golding's classic *Lord of the Flies*—a book to bury in any time capsule seeking to convey the flavour of this half of the century. In Richard Hughes's *High Wind in Jamaica,* in Rumer Godden's *The Greengage Summer,* and of course Nabokov's *Lolita,* children collude erotically with adults, and even betray them; in

Doris Lessing's *The Fifth Child,* the evil baby actually wrecks a stable family. Popular satanist entertainment, including *Rosemary's Baby, The Exorcist, Poltergeist,* build on Christian theories of demonic possession to dramatise the full-blown development of evil in seeming cherubim. Gone are the cheerful catapults and squashed toffees and fallen socks of a scallywag like Just William, the devilry of Dennis the Menace. Horror has spread into teenage fiction, too, with titles like *The Babysitter, The Burning Baby,* and *Dance of the Scalpel.*

Although the cultural and social investment in childhood innocence is constantly tested by experience, and assailed by doubts, it's still continued to grow. As psychoanalytical understanding of children's sexuality has deepened, so have attempts to contain it. The duration of the age of expected innocence has been greatly extended since Victorian times, for instance: a good thing, if it can prevent exploiting child labour and adult molestation but perhaps not, in other cases.

Most teenagers will have broken at least one of the many laws that forbid them adult behaviour—like smoking, drinking, clubbing, watching X-rated films or having sex—thus placing them willy-nilly outside the law, and helping to reconfirm their identity as intrinsically delinquent anyway (something they don't find entirely uncongenial, of course).

At the same time, the notion of child sexuality is encoded in upbringing at a much younger age than before. The modern emphasis on sex difference, on learning masculinity and femininity, begins with the clothing of the infants, and has developed markedly since the end of the First World War. A boy who was dressed in pink ribbons by his father today would very likely be taken away from his care. Yet Robert Louis Stevenson, whose character was hardly disturbed, appears in a daguerreotype around the age of three dressed in fur-trimmed cape, full skirts, hair slide and spit curls; a photograph album in the Victoria and Albert Museum from the beginning of the century shows a boy child on his birthday every year—ringletted from curling papers, full-skirted, with button boots. The portraits of the French or English aristocracy and gentry showing children clothed as adults, with jewels and powdered wigs and crinolines and far-thingales, were displaying the status of their families; but the little girl in the little black dress, patent pumps, lipstick and earrings who was brought out in the finale of a recent Chanel collection was showing off her body, and looked like a travesty of the sex-free youth children are supposed to enjoy.

Yet even if children today aren't titillatingly dressed, they can still be looked at salaciously. It's we who have lost innocent eyes, we who can only be ironical children. Lewis Carroll's friends were undisturbed by his photographs of their children, while some pederasts today, it seems, are kept very happy by Mothercare catalogues.

Pornography clusters to the sacred and the forbidden like wasps' nests in chimneys: and children have in many ways replaced women. The very term child abuse, of recent, highly symptomatic coinage, implies that there's a proper use for children, and it is not sexual. Yet at the same time, there circulates more disguised kiddie porn than at any other period in history, and more speculation about their internal lives of fantasy and desire. The nineteenth century used *femmes fatales* with bedroom eyes and trailing tresses, wetlook drapery and floating chiffon on their official buildings and advertisements, but the late twentieth century has seen children emerge as the principal incitements to desire: the nymph or the vamp has yielded pride of place to the nymphet, the urchin and the toddler.

There's probably no way out of this maze of mirrors, at least on this side of eternity, unless, like Islam, we were to ban graven images—especially of children as objects of desire. The consecration of childhood raises the real-life examples of children to an ideal which they must fail, modestly by simply being ordinary kids, or horrendously by becoming victims or criminals. But childhood doesn't occupy some sealed Eden or Neverland set apart from the grown-up world: our children can't be better than we are.

Children have never been so visible as points of identification, as warrants of virtue, as markers of humanity. Yet the quality of their lives has been deteriorating for a good fifteen years in this and many other Western countries; in England and the United States, one of the fastest-growing groups living in poverty are children and their mothers. The same ministers who sneer about babies on benefit, and trumpet a return to basic values cannot see that our social survival as a civilised community depends on stopping this spiralling impoverishment of children's lives. In the UK alone, the Child Poverty Action Group estimates that a third of all children are suffering from an unacceptably low standard of living. Of the million jobs to be created in this country between now and the year 2000, 90 percent —yes, 90 percent will be for women, according to one official forecast. And yet there's publicly funded child care for only 2 per cent of under-threes. Meanwhile, the government's proposed to allocate £100 million to creating prisons for eleven- to thirteen-year old offenders.

To add to the difficulties, economic individualism has brought us the ultimate nightmare—not just the child as commodity, but the child consumer. Plenty of dinosaur lunchboxes at school, not many books in the library. The wicked, greedy, knowing child grows in the same ground as the industry around childhood innocence: children are expensive to raise, anyway, but all the products made for them unashamedly appeal to their pester power—as consumers of films, hamburgers, the right brand of sneakers, video games. The child, as a focus of worship, has been privatised as an economic unit, has become a link in the circulation of money and desire.

That very vitality of imagination so envied in children needs to be tended—and not only by expensive theme parks. Yet the BBC uproots the tradition of children's radio at a stroke, citing falling ratings. And in the same playgrounds where Peter and Iona Opie collected the skipping songs and hopscotch rhymes of generations, children apparently now hang around, having forgotten how to play. Local, oral traditions are dropping away just like larks and hedges. I'm not turning into a reactionary Little England ruralist—but children's songs flourish in context, in conditions when children can play together in groups in safety. At present, playgrounds and other school facilities—among the only safe spaces for children—are routinely left idle after school hours, at weekends and during holidays for want of funds to staff them.

Fallow playgrounds are a tiny aspect of the disgrace: the hours that British men work are longer than almost all of their counterparts in Europe. And yet the cry goes up about children with only mothers to look after them. Children with fathers who live with them aren't looked after by them either, even when they would like to, since employment is still structured to consider childcare the mother's task. And measures which would grant fathers paternity and sickness leave on behalf of their children are rejected because they might jeopardise profits.

Many of these problems result from the concept that childhood and adult life are separate when they are in effect inextricably intertwined. Children aren't separate from adults, and unlike Mowgli or Peter Pan, can't be kept separate; they can't live innocent lives on behalf of adults, like medieval hermits maintained at court by libertine kings to pray for them, or the best china kept in tissue in the cupboard. Nor can individuals who happen to be young act as the living embodiments of adults' inner goodness, however much adults may wish it. Without paying attention to adults and their circumstances, children cannot begin to meet the hopes and expectations of our torn dreams about what a child and childhood should be. Children are our copy, in little: in Pol Pot's Cambodia they'll denounce their own families; in affluent cities of the West, they'll wail for expensive sneakers with the right label like their friend's. The one thing that can be said for absolute certain about children is that they're very quick to learn.

We know by now that the man is father to the child; we fear that children will grow up to be even more like us than they already are. Caspar Hauser the innocent was murdered; now we're scared that if such a wild child were to appear today he might kill us.

FOUR

BEAUTIFUL BEASTS

The Call of the Wild

A length of rope, made of steel wire at one end, can be interwoven with jute fiber until the other end of the rope is altogether different, and yet it'll still be the same rope, unbroken from end to end. Within today's myths of human nature, the warrior and the wild creature, the child and the beast don't stand at opposite ends, but are intertwined, continuous, inseparable. And yet they're in polar opposition to one another, too. In the argument about the difference between humans and animals, there's been a pronounced change of sympathy, growing ever more strongly since the eighteenth century. And it's the wild pole that has been radiating the greater magnetic attraction on human imagination and allegiance.

In the medieval romance *Valentine and Orson,* the Empress

of Constantinople finds herself alone in a wild forest giving birth to twins. Her husband, the Emperor, has cruelly cast her out under false suspicion of adultery. A passing she-bear steals one of the children for herself; the other baby, Valentine, is rescued with his mother when a nobleman comes riding by at the right moment and takes them both home with him. This twin, Valentine, grows up at court, to become a valiant prince, while the lost boy, Orson, or Bear Cub, grows up 'a wild hairy man, doing great mischief to all that pass[ed] through the forest.'

The separated twins' tumultuous legend tells how the brothers later meet and fight and how Valentine captures the Wild Man Orson. At Valentine's side, Orson overcomes giants and even conquers the Green Knight himself. He receives baptism, but his wild nature persists: his pelt stands in for clothes, he's shaggy, unkempt, and roars incoherently at the top of his voice. The pair, now sworn companions, sally forth on more adventures, and yet more, against the infidel. A magic oracle in the shape of a brazen head tells them who they are, and they realise their affinity runs deeper than mere comradeship, that they are twins by blood. At this point, Orson acquires the use of his tongue for other purposes besides great war cries. Trials of strength follow, doughty deeds, mighty battles against foes far and wide—until at last Valentine dies to leave Orson to retire back into the wilderness—but at this last stage of his turbulent career, in the form of a hermit.

The romance *Valentine and Orson* was translated from a lost French original by Henry Watson and printed by Caxton's successor Wynkyn de Worde at the beginning of the sixteenth century. It has been reprinted many times in different adaptations, including a dynamic full-color version by the pioneering Victorian illustrator Walter Crane, and a recent retelling for children by Nancy Ekholm Burkert. But it seems to be almost forgotten today, even though the story of the twin brothers, one wild, one tame, gives precious clues to historical attitudes to nature and reveals the changing relationship between human and animal.

In *Valentine and Orson,* the bear child becomes civilised, attains rationality and humanity at the hands of his human brother. His passage into the realm of Art, Culture, and Society takes place, in a version written around 1835, when he's captured— by guile, for Valentine couldn't of course overcome him by force:

> At the first dawn of morning, Valentine arose, and putting on his armour, took a shield polished like a mirror, and having arrived at the forest, he climbed a high tree near the bear's cave. Presently he heard Orson, who had a buck with him which he had just killed, come roaring by; and he could not help admiring the beauty of his make, and his agility, wishing it were possible to tame him. He then tore off a branch of a tree, and threw it at Orson, who, looking up, uttered a furious howl, and darted up the tree like lightning. Valentine descended, and Orson, seeing him on the ground, rushed down . . . Valentine, [held] up his shield, [and] Orson, evidently surprised and delighted, beheld his own image.

Just as Perseus used Medusa's mask to free Andromeda from the monster, so Valentine spellbinds the wild man: in this version, he's 'delighted' with his reflection, and becomes docile, but in others, he's alarmed by his own wild aspect. In both cases, he's unmanned by new self-consciousness. Taking advantage of this, Valentine then attacks the she-bear, Orson's mother, but Orson leaps to her defence; Valentine gives the bear strong liquor to sozzle her—the drink's so potent and she so unused to it, it kills her instantly. Orson, desperate with grief, surrenders to Valentine.

The scene of Orson's capture borrows the advice of medieval bestiaries on hunting a tigress. To catch that wildest of wild beasts, the hunter should throw down a glass globe in the animal's path; she'll see herself reflected in it in miniature and mistake her image for her cub; this will stop her in her tracks, and she'll try to pick it up, giving the huntsman time to drop a net over her.

The story doesn't allow Orson to remain 'savage'; he enters his brother's culture, and this is quickly marked by an improvement in his table manners. When first brought to court, on a leash like a beast, 'he tore the fowls asunder with his claws, and devoured them like a ravenous wolf, and then thrusting his head into a cistern of water he drank as much as might have sufficed a horse.' But Valentine soon teaches him the use of a glass and a fork. These accomplishments don't decrease Orson's amazing strength: he still performs extraordinary feats on behalf of his brother and the Christian cause. Though he retains the character of a brute, in his wild skins and his incoherent speech, these also signify natural innocence, like the camel hide of John the Baptist in the desert, and the penitential veil of hair worn by Mary Magdalene. They signal, too, the corresponding rejection of artifice, of civilisation, of worldly vanities, in short of human culture as the carrier of an intrinsic sinfulness. The twin boys Valentine and Orson stand for polarised goals—an 1822 edition for children put it straightforwardly: 'In Valentine we contemplate a man endowed with the education of Art, whilst the person and character of Orson discover the simple workings of Nature.'

Few Elizabethans would have considered themselves kin to a crocodile, or thought of adopting an endangered species to prevent its extinction. In Elizabeth I's time, a courtier, bespattered with the blood foaming from the lips of a bear at a bear-baiting session, rejoiced in the sport; the early French rationalist, Descartes, arrived at the firm analysis that an animal was merely a machine—natural, but lacking a soul. As we all know, our evolutionary proximity to the apes caused horror in the last century. Adam had been lord of creation in the Bible, and named the beasts; now he was merely one of their kind. The peacock no longer existed simply to delight his eyes, or the pig to fill his belly.

Of course cruelty to animals continues, and identification with them is sporadic and inconsistent. But zoos, where people thrilled to see wild creatures in the last century, are now closing down or turning into show farms with domestic animals only. Circuses with animal acts are largely doomed, even when the performers aren't wild creatures, but dogs and ponies. A protester has died at a hunt meeting, in an accident with the van bringing in the hounds; a father has placed his son on the racetrack of the Grand National to prevent cruelty to the horses. Campaigns to save whales, seals, dolphins, spiders—and crocodiles—attract enormous followings, and have had some real effect on hunting and trading practices. The desire for closeness to animal power may still stimulate the breeding of fighting dogs, but it also drives the rise in the variety of soft toys. Not only the teddy bear, but many kinds of reptiles and scary animals—and dinosaurs—are now transformed by plush and stuffing into reassuring, cuddly, domestic gods, nursery talismans.

The symbolic value of wild animals has ancient, tough mythological roots and these are intertwined with the definition of humanity's virtue—virtue in the sense of both goodness and potency. Even when despised in an anthropocentric world, wild things have offered a standard by which human identity and exploits could be measured: their proximity often proves a legendary hero's strength, *The Greek Alexander* romance, extant since the third century AD, is a hugely entertaining farrago of history, tall stories, and esoteric wisdom. It exalts its hero, Alexander the Great, by staging a sequence of confrontations with monsters of the wilds. His heroism doesn't only consist in conquest and extermination, but in taming and incorporation: wild things aren't monsters to the same degree as Medusa or Chimaera—they're barbaric rather than alien.

The picaresque narrative follows Alexander to the borders of the known world and beyond, from where he writes a letter home, to his mother:

> We set out and came to a green country where . . . we saw a huge man with hair all over his body, and we were frightened. I gave orders to capture him. When he was taken he gazed at us ferociously. I ordered a naked woman to be brought to him; but he grabbed her and ate her. The soldiers rushed up to rescue her, but he made a gnashing noise with his teeth. The rest of the natives heard him, and came running towards us out of the swamp: there were about 10,000 of them . . . I ordered the swamp to be set alight; and when they saw the fire they fled . . . They had no human intelligence, but barked like dogs.

Alexander routs the wild men with fire, sign of the hearth and culture, in the same way as Valentine used another symbol of consciousness—the mirror—to prevail over his wild brother. More familiar heroes who had to contend with—and master—the wild include Hercules, father to many a superman. He overcame the Nemean lion and plenty of other wild creatures. Centuries on and rather closer to home, Max, in Maurice Sendak's exhilarating children's story, puts on his wolf suit, visits the land Where the Wild Things Are, joins in their wild rumpus and becomes their king—before he comes back home to his supper and finds it still hot.

Sometimes the distinction between taming the beast and becoming one of them is blurred, as in the case of Max. Many a classical deity or warrior has been raised by animals in the wilds—Zeus was suckled by Amaltheia, a nymph in the form of a she-goat, and fed with wild honey from combs found in the hollow of a tree, as can be seen in a wonderfully vigorous painting in the Dulwich Collection. Poussin's sometimes frozen poetry appears here to be itself molten with sap and sweetness. The healer god Asclepius was also abandoned, and nursed by a she-goat, and guarded by a sheepdog. The legendary founders of Rome, Romulus and Remus, were rescued by a she-wolf after being exposed on a mountainside; such legends survive in heraldry, and some English, French or Italian families claim descent from the union of an ancestor with a wild thing—like the Orsini, whose ancestor, as their name suggests, was reared by a bear.

The animal mother breaks the link with human parents, she helps distinguish her charge from ordinary children, she confers on him a mark of special difference from the human. The she-goat or bear or wolf nourishes the man of destiny with her vitality—presented, in such stories, as somehow more vital than a human mother's milk, as intrinsically natural with a capital N—the forest, not the city, the raw, not the cooked, the wild, not the tame. While attitudes to Nature historically oscillate in a complex pattern of praise and dread, the mythic hero is often represented as achieving the union of nature and culture in his person, both in his origin and in his exploits. But the difficulty of this synthesis becomes part of the agonistic struggle the narrative of heroism relates—and sometimes a tragic part.

The *Epic of Gilgamesh,* written in Sumer around five thousand years ago, foreshadows the twins Valentine and Orson when it confronts the urban warlord Gilgamesh, King of Uruk, with the wild forest dweller Enkidu. Enkidu has been made by the goddess from clay dropped in the wilderness:

There was virtue in him of the god of war... His body was rough, he had long hair like a woman's... [He] was covered with matted hair like Samuqan's, the god of cattle. He was innocent of mankind; he knew nothing of cultivated land.

Enkidu ate grass in the hills with the gazelle and jostled with wild beasts at the water-holes; he had joy of the water with the herds of wild game.

Gilgamesh captures him, using a harlot as bait; the seductions of the woman subdue the wild man, and he's led, docile, into the city. At first Gilgamesh and Enkidu fight, 'they grappled, holding each other like bulls. They broke the doorposts and the walls shook, they snorted like bulls locked together.' But then, they recognise that they're a true match for each other; this is literally meant, with the full force of the word, match: though different in appearance, origin, conduct, they feel a twinship, and become boon companions, beloved friends, the first buddies in literature. Until Enkidu is killed—and descends into the underworld, where Gilgamesh follows him but can't pull him back to life. In this ancient poem, the hero takes the wild man to himself, binds him in love to his life, but inevitably fails to incorporate him totally; if he managed, the wild man would no longer be what he is. Gilgamesh finds himself condemned to lament this impossibility and his loss for as long as he lives. It's perhaps intrinsic to the nature of wild hairy Enkidu that in order to retain his integrity, he must resist such dominion. He represents an attachment to the innocence of mankind, symbolised by his oneness with nature, and it can't be maintained within city walls; this loss haunts the poem in which he appears, and the same loss continues to haunt philosophy, storytelling, mythmaking, and ideas about maleness, never perhaps more so than today. The threat of entropy in nature, brought about by human achievements—by the car, the aerosol, the nuclear reactor, pesticides, and genetic interference—has never been so serious nor perhaps—even in times of millennial fever—so acutely felt. Nature, newly understood to be somehow uncontaminated, innocent, nurturing and spontaneous, beckons as a remedy to the distortions and excesses of progress. In the popular comic strip, green Ninja Turtles do battle with computer nerds who threaten earth with ecocatastrophe.

The wild man has been invoked as a healing figure for today's ills by more and more different groups: environmental campaigners, New Age believers, and enthusiasts of local folklore. In South Queensferry in Scotland, at the Annual August fair, a figure called the Burry Man walks through the town, bearing great sceptres of harvest fruits and foliage in both hands and is greeted as he goes with offerings of flowers and money. Completely parcelled up in forty-two mats made of burdock burrs and brown paper, until only his eyes peep out of a prickly mask, he looks like a nubbly hedgehog; paraded in silence all day, seven miles through the town, he's thought to assure fruitfulness—in this predominantly fishing community, to fill the nets. Though the custom is presented as hallowed by great and mysterious antiquity, the earliest record of his procession dates from 1746. The word folklore itself was only coined a hundred years later, and like many folklore practices with pagan undertones, the Burry Man has become more and more entrenched in the last twenty years—ironically just as the burdock weed itself becomes more and more scarce. Local loyalties play their part: the Burry Man personifies the spirit of the place, even wearing a Scottish lion rampant round his middle; but he also corresponds in function to Enkidu or Orson, harnessing the energy of nature at a time when this is felt to be more and more needed.

But spirits of plenty like the Burry Man don't help untangle the contemporary anxiety about the place of human beings in the natural order. And the rise in green consciousness has gotten muddled, when it comes to the human animal, with a celebration of wildness, interpreted as an ideal of energy—sexual, unrepressed, and individualist. When advertisers feature a bear, a mountain lion, an ibex, or other wild things to endorse the life-giving properties of a car, alcohol, mineral water or shampoo, they're also communicating an idea of heroic and untrammelled independence—free spirits. Social animals hardly have selling power (besides they're mostly insects, or rodents, or uneasy birds like rooks) and are not endangered. The lone hero, the pattern of modern man, finds an image of himself under threat of extinction in the large mammals, the gorilla, the grizzly, and the lynx.

Some useful earlier distinctions have been blurred by this nostalgic desire for the power and freedom of the wild. Metamorphosis out of human shape into another, beastly form used to express a fall from human grace. The first metamorphosis in Ovid's great book picks up on a familiar modern myth that even

Plato mentioned in *The Republic*. Lycaon, ruler of Arcadia, kills and cooks a hostage. For this lack of hospitality, Zeus turns him into the first werewolf. Callisto is changed into a little bear by Hera in revenge for the love Zeus feels for her; Circe mockingly degrades Odysseus's men when she changes them into swine.

Milton gives their brutishness the full edge of his scorn in his play, *Comus*:

> *. . . their human countenance,*
> *The express resemblance of the gods, is changed*
> *Into some brutish form of wolf, or bear,*
> *Or ounce [lynx], of tiger, hog, or bearded goat . . .*
> *And they so perfect in their misery,*
> *Not once perceive their foul disfigurement,*
> *But boast themselves more comely than before,*
> *And all their friends and native home forget,*
> *To roll with pleasure in a sensual sty.*

Like beasts, like Orson before he knows Valentine's mirror, they have no capacity for that self-consciousness which spells human identity.

In the parallel, predominantly Christian tradition, such animal mutations were the work of the devil. Indeed, as fairy tales often evolve out of religious stories, the defeat of an ogre like Bluebeard recapitulates many comforting Christian tales about women who unwittingly marry the devil but, with the help of the Virgin Mary, free themselves in the end from his binding charms. Even Bluebeard's name contains a memory of the shaggy-hair'd blue devils of the Bible, represented in stained-glass windows and on the mystery play stage, where they would caper with firecrackers gripped between their teeth.

St Thomas Aquinas analysed the devil's tricks and suggested that the animal metamorphoses he performed consisted of three types of illusion: the devil could tamper with someone's vision so that they saw monsters where there were none; or he could fashion an apparition; or, thirdly, the devil could change someone into an animal like a wolf or a black cat.

The various Beast-shapes which unsavoury lovers take in fairy tale often communicate women storytellers' jaundiced view of marriage; animal shape denotes animal lust, above all. In *The Ram* by Madame d'Aulnoy, for instance, written at the turn of the seventeenth century, the princess-heroine simply leaves her husband the ram to die, while she busies herself taking charge of her father's kingdom. Significantly, another of Madame d'Aulnoy's heroines comes across a whole circle of hell peopled with men in enchanted animal shape, and discovers that they have been punished for various marital crimes, for wife-beating, rape, and so forth, and that their shape corresponds to these offences.

The forms which the devil adopted also coincidentally reproduced actual threats to people and livestock in times of famine when wolves and even bears entered the villages from their lairs in the wild. Tales about such predators didn't need to grow in the telling: there's a ring of genuine terror in the report of the Dutch mariners who, in 1597, looking for the northern passage to China, found the pack ice closing in and the phantom shapes of polar bears hovering waiting to pounce on the dying crew.

It's blithely symptomatic of contemporary forgettings that we now find bears sweet. The return to human form used to be the quest, the reward, the reason of the fairy tale in the first place. But beastly shape is now becoming an appealing alternative, even a prize, a more valuable rather than a degraded state. The beast seems to offer a refuge from the robot.

Listen to the scene setting of a recent video game called 'Altered Beast':

It is the time of gods and myths and legends. When men were warriors and courageously fought unnatural enemies in the endless battle of good against evil. It is the time of the Altered Beast . . . Although you were once a brave and awesome Roman Centurion, the rigors of this journey demand a supernatural display of strength. So you are bestowed with the powers of the Altered Beast. The power to transform your being into a part-animal, part-human creature of formidable force.

As you advance through the levels and perils of the game, you—former soldier—mutate into various animals, all of them capable of great mischief, like Enkidu, like Orson: first a werewolf, next a were dragon, a were bear, and at last, a gold werewolf, in which guise you can defeat the ogre and rescue Athena—wisdom—whom he's been holding captive.

This load of old cobblers is very interesting because the game's metamorphoses are running counter to the traditional current of Western myth and folklore, in which the human absorbs the animal by taming it and mastering it. Even more fundamentally, it contradicts the underlying value of the Gilgamesh-Enkidu, Valentine-Orson pairings, that the human hero remains superior however deep his reliance on his beastly ally, however urgent his attachment. The new myth of the wild calls into question the privilege of being a human at all. The video game catches well the prevailing tendency of mythic heroism: the metamorphoses, all into the beastly, choose exactly the same predators that terrorise the protagonists in fairy tales like Red Riding Hood.

This new assignation of higher value to wild creatures gains force when there's a woman in the picture. The seductress sets alight inherent sensuality, which in these stories is coded animal. But the value of this animal wildness grows by contrast to the domesticating threat of women's love. For in this type of myth, women represent—most unusually—the domain of culture, and culture becomes the enemy of nature's glorious, powerful, unrestrained energies. In the *Epic of Gilgamesh*, as we saw, the harlot is sent out from the city to trap Enkidu, and succeeds in gentling him with her charms; the energy of the wild figure in myth, when it meets a woman, transmutes into desire which can prove the undoing of the wild elements in his nature—this in turn can make or break him.

The change of attitude over time to this encounter can be seen very clearly in the different ways the ancient fairy tale of Beauty and the Beast has been told. The Beast presents the major mythic figure of masculine potency, of Eros, and the plots in which he moves offer a blueprint for the proper channelling of masculine erotic energy in society; this alters according to context. Until rather recently, the Beast suffered from his disfigurement; sometimes it expressed just punishment for earlier bad behaviour. Under the evil spell, the Beast fears that nobody will ever love him in this form and he'll never be freed. Even as late as the Cocteau film of 1946, for instance, the Beast feels himself doomed in his beastliness. Against his will, he hunts wild creatures and tears them limb from limb to devour them raw; his great claws and mane smoulder after a kill. He can only speak monosyllabically to La Belle, and his brutishness repels her. La Belle will release him, eventually, from this confining, animal realm through those human qualities of mercy and love.

Enchanting as the film is, and fascinating as the Beast's charms are, Cocteau's film was already quaint in its symbolist allegiance to the redemptive powers of civility—of art and beauty and romance.

Many earlier, popular versions of the story show, by contrast, a marked preference for the Beast. And the most familiar and revealing example is *King Kong,* the monster movie of all time, which was made in 1933 and has proved, alongside *The Wizard of Oz,* one of Hollywood's highest earners. *King Kong* gives a new spin to the old tale when it opens with the lugubrious prophecy: 'And lo, the beast looked upon the face of beauty. And it stayed its hand from killing. And from that day, it was as one dead.' The plot unfolds how an intrepid aventurer, Carl Denham, has heard about a prodigious mystery, the 'Eighth Wonder of the World'.

Everything about Kong places him in direct succession to the monstrous wild men of myth and legend. Homo Sylvestris was the name of the 'missing link' between the brute and the human and was imagined by some early palaeontologists as a species of upright orangutan, a great ape. Kong's jungle kingdom, sealed behind a fortified wall and massive gates, exists beyond the borders of the known world, on an island recorded only by one sea captain who is now dead. The island, once it comes into view, all precipitous cliffs and hulking doomy crags, was significantly modelled on Gustave Doré's engravings for *Paradise Lost*—and it's pertinent that Doré's Bible had also inspired early reconstructions of primitive man. The creatures who live there belong in a lost world, before history, before civilisation: the jungle is filled with giant predators, man-eating pterodactyls and Loch Ness monsters who gobble up several members of the crew. Kong's worshippers, first signalling their presence by frenzied drumming, appear daubed and arrayed in feathers, bones, furs, grass skirts, ornaments—anything, Aztec, Zulu, New Guinea or Hawaiian, to create a fetishized fiction of savagery. Cavorting and stomping, they're seen preparing a young bride to sacrifice her to the monster: the scene has every look and sound of the savage rites in fantasy literature of exploration and empire.

The filmmakers, Merian C. Cooper and Ernest Schoedsack, took as their motto 'the three D's—distance, danger and difficulty'. The pair were air force veterans, later turned mercenaries and buccaneers. Theirs was a boy's own ethic, rip-roaring, macho, empire building, showy: in the famous final scene, when Kong on the top of the Empire State Building is attacked from the air, the director and his producer filmed themselves piloting the planes that shoot at Kong. However, in the film's closing words, the death of Kong is given in a different version: 'No, it wasn't the aeroplanes; it was Beauty killed the Beast.' Again, as in the *Epic of Gilgamesh,* a woman has been used as bait, a blonde—the actress Fay Wray, who after her performance in this film became the first of the adored 'screamers' of Hollywood.

The film begins by firmly establishing a primordial, savage king of the jungle—the beast Kong. But, after Fay Wray's abduction, the film begins to sway sympathies in another direction: fear and loathing gradually change to identification. Sexuality moves to the centre of the story and the great ape becomes a figure of a man, a desiring, aspiring, frustrated, tragic male. When Kong doesn't eat Fay Wray, or violate her, but carries her off to a rocky height—anticipating the last sequence on an urban pinnacle—and then examines her, the audience is caught up in his wonder at her flimsy delicacy in his great paw; the scene was censored in 1938, for its sexual intimacy: it shows Kong picking off a filmy sliver of skirt and then sniffing his fingers, with twitching nostrils as the music turns soft and tender.

Later, when Kong's put on show in New York, cruciform on a gallows as if at a slave auction, he becomes an emblem of civilisation's savagery. His animal wildness shows up the limitations of human culture; when he thinks the exploding flashbulbs of the cameras are going to harm Fay Wray, he breaks his shackles. His freedom rampage through the city—in pursuit of the blonde—then begins.

King Kong turns into an ironical critique of human society, of its cruelty and greed and love of show; the sympathy it displays towards the beast rather than the beauty grows stronger throughout, however illogically, until the climactic end. When Carl Denham first captured Kong, stunning him with gas bombs, he ordered him to be tied up and cried out, 'We'll give him more than chains . . . we'll teach him Fear.' The chains, the fear, mark the end of his wild days: repression, domestication. At the start, the monster represents nature versus humanity; by the end, he dramatises a worse danger for men: women. The crushing of Kong becomes just another episode in the long tragic chronicle about male libidos unjustly slapped down. Fay Wray's rejection of him inaugurates a rich tradition in popular culture, of sympathetic monsters spurned. Such plots neatly manage a stack of pleasures: they flatter women with evidence of their remarkable powers to excite and tame the primitive, they excuse men their deep-down wild impulses—and explain their failure to gratify them. At the same time, the story upholds the terror of predatory male power because that justifies the need for chivalrous vengeance and continual control of women: it's a rescue romance, and there's nothing else for Fay Wray to do but scream like a terrified child.

But even while she screams, she never quite quells the idea that all beauties deep down really want a beast: that Kong might be the monster of her dreams.

In the recent Disney cartoon film, *Beauty and the Beast,* there are two beasts. Both are suitors for Belle's love, and it's the one in human shape who loses out: Gaston, the hunky beefcake, a Sylvester Stallone lookalike, falls to a horrible and well-deserved death of the precipice at the Beast's castle. But as for Belle's lover in animal form—half Minotaur, half lion—Belle attends to his personal growth. He learns to weep, not roar, and wins her through his cultural attributes, especially his amazingly well-stocked library. Unlike Gaston, he doesn't go hunting and shooting; he's aware of his shortcomings, and grieves like a good existentialist at his condition. The film promises its audience Prince Charming will turn out a New Man, virile yet tender, natural yet cultivated, in touch with his emotions, childlike in the best sense, yet mature and responsible in his attitude. All he needed was the love of a good woman. This is a woman's film: the script is by Linda Woolverton, and it shows throughout that it has in mind an audience of mums and daughters. It's an ingenious attempt to negotiate the very tricky ground to women's attraction to male appetite.

But the animators invest the Beast with such allure that they can't find a way to bring him back to humankind without bathos. After the Beast, Prince Charming can only be a comedown.

Angela Carter wrote several dazzling variations of the Beauty and the Beast tale in her collection *The Bloody Chamber,* and challenged the tradition of taming, or civilising, or otherwise containing the Beast. In 'The Tiger's Bride', she turns the traditional ending upside down, and it's Beauty who metamorphoses, shedding her human shape in the last lines of the story:

He dragged himself closer and closer to me, until I felt the harsh velvet of his head against my hand, then a tongue, abrasive as sandpaper. 'He will lick the skin off me!'

And each stroke of his tongue ripped off skin after successive skin, all the skins of a life in the world, and left behind a nascent patina of shining hairs. My earrings turned back to water and trickled down my shoulders; I shrugged the drops off my beautiful fur.

It's too easy to dismiss visions of the beast's newfound nobility as male self-flattery, or even, more seriously, as sentimental justifications of toughness, brute strength, independence—the same stuff of the warrior. The beast, the wildman Enkidu, and the bear cub Orson issue exciting invitations to a journey, to pleasure. Their domain can't be the exclusive property of one sex. In modern myth, it's not that the boundary has been eroded between human and animal—rather, the value given to each side in the contrast has changed. And contemporary stories are finding a way to answer the call of the wild.

FIVE

CANNIBAL TALES

The Hunger for Conquest

In 1844, the great Victorian art historian and critic John Ruskin was given a painting by his father as a reward for the success of the first volume of his book *Modern Painters*. It was a picture by Turner, and Ruskin admired it above all others, writing of it: 'I believe, if I were reduced to rest Turner's immortality upon any single work, I should choose this.' Ruskin kept the painting for nearly twenty-five years, until he found the subject, he said, too painful, and had to part with it. Before that he had evoked his Turner in one of his most gorgeous hymns to the sublime:

> . . . purple and blue, the lurid shadows of the hollow break-
> ers are cast upon the mist of night, which gathers cold and
> low, advancing like the shadow of death upon the guilty

ship as it labours amidst the lightning of the sea, its thin masts written upon the sky in lines of blood, girded with condemnation in that fearful hue which signs the sky with horror, and mixes its flowing flood with the sunlight, and, cast far along the desolate heave of the sepulchral waves, incarnadines the multitudinous sea.

In all this welter of praise, Ruskin never tackled the subject of the painting at all. It's usually known as 'The Slave Ship', but its full title is 'Slavers throwing overboard the dead and dying— Typhon coming on'. In the foreground, the drowning slaves are just visible, while shoals of sea monsters are racing towards them to gorge on them.

Turner had been reading a study of the British struggle for the abolition of slavery and found that in 1783 the owners and captain of a ship called the *Zong* were charged with fraud by an insurance company. They had claimed for the deaths of a cargo of slaves by drowning. The policy didn't cover death from illness, and so the captain had thrown overboard, on three successive days, a hundred and twenty-two sick men and women in order to collect the money for them. The insurance company proved their case. No further criminal proceedings, however, were instituted by the courts against the *Zong*'s masters.

Turner painted this extraordinary synthesis of the trade's horror seven years after the abolition of slavery. His approach sublimates the theme: the drowning scarcely appear. One black leg, shackled at the ankle, breaks the surface of the seething water like a splintered spar in the foreground; alongside, pairs of hands are raised to make imploring gestures which rhyme—with ghastly irony—the fins of many fish cresting the waves as they arrive for the feast. Huge links of chain thrash in the water, rather implausibly, but marking the position of submerged bodies below. Turner was always more interested in the weather than in people, and he gives us just the one leg, waving hands, and the great glassy visage and gaping maw of the sea monsters.

Turner's symbolic approach to the tragedy was later mirrored in Ruskin's evasiveness. Ruskin suggests a crime, and cannot bring himself to name it: the ship is 'guilty', the murderous deeds of Macbeth haunt his prose, bloodshed stains the sea. But he never faces the issues of race and power which the painting raises. Instead, he's vague: 'the whole picture', he wrote, '[is] dedicated to the most sublime of subjects and impressions . . . the power, majesty and deathfulness of the open, deep, illimitable sea.'

The sea has played a central role in the making of British identity, and Turner is of course its most passionate painter, as well as one of the most conscious patriots ever to paint (his eccentric will named as his heirs 'Poor and Decayed Male Artists'—but they had to be born in England, of legally wed English parents). In 'The Slave Ship', Turner is reflecting on the passing of that grandeur of spirit he saw in Britain's rule, that glorious adventure and mastery which the empire represented round the world. The picture is an elegy—for a lost vision and perhaps an ideal, too. The victims are there, not for their own sakes as protagonists, but as witnesses. Yet what is of acute interest is that Turner gives so many different strokes and colours to the single metaphor of consuming and being consumed, devouring and being devoured.

The dazzling wake of sunset and its reflection, which cleaves the painting in two, itself resembles a kind of parted mouth, open for swallowing. But consuming retains its mercantile meaning, too. Turner added some lines from a poem he'd written when he sent the picture to the Royal Academy in 1840:

Hope, Hope, fallacious Hope!
Where is thy market now?

The bodies in the water are goods, destined for market, and now spoiled, the false hope is the trader's hope for profit. Turner's whiskered, jowly, and even pink sea monsters moving in to feed on flesh stand for the well-fed but still hungry, pink, whiskery merchants who trade in Africans. He identifies himself with them—the slavers are his first-person subjects, not the dead and dying, the slaves. And behind the slavers lingers the shadow of Turner and his own kind—he writes those lines of the poem, however bitterly, in the voice of the profiteer who has lost his cargo.

Something else is also hinted by the imagery of the marine feast in the painting: an allusion to the deep-seated racial myth of cannibalism, to the much-repeated notion that the people who were sold as slaves were not of humankind. And the most laconic sign of the not-human had been since classical times, cannibalism. Those cannibal fish, representing the slave traders, bring to mind the question Montaigne put three hundred years earlier, when he asked, who were the barbarians: Christians who hanged, drew and quartered their fellows, tortured them with irons and burned them alive at the stake, or savages who waited till their victims were dead before they cooked them? Turner's painting raises a similar doubt: Who are the cannibals now, us or them?

Above all, the painting also communicates the way history forgets: the bodies which aren't visible any longer will indeed be consigned to oblivion, will be consumed partly by wonder at the paint effects, as in Ruskin's response, partly by the difficulties later viewers will experience in confronting the story told. Like the law, they'd rather drop the case.

But the imagination doesn't blank out; its characteristic movement tends to write graffiti on any empty space. Without telling the particular story, a generic one will expand to fill the gap. Cannibalism has become more salient today as a modern myth, easily fulfilling myth's multiple functions, defining the forbidden and the alluring, the sacred and the profane, conjuring demons and heroes, saying who we are and what we want, telling a story which makes sense of things. Cannibalism has become popular myth, turning up in the chilly arthouse aesthetic of Peter Greenaway's cinema, and in thrillers like *Silence of the Lambs*. Hannibal Lecter—Cannibal Lecher—has become such a famous character, that like a myth, he's larger than the story which produced him. Gallows humour, in comic horror films like *Delicatessen* and even stage musicals, offers one way of speaking the unspeakable: Sweeney Todd, featuring the demon barber who ate his victims in meat pies, included a jolly flesh-eating duet and became an international hit.

Cannibal stories are still widespread. The *Independent on Sunday* recently introduced a feature about New Guinea with the words: 'Now the Yali go to church . . . But it isn't long since some of the missionaries were eaten.' Needless to say, on reading the article it's clear that no one the author—Norman Lewis—talked to had ever eaten anyone—it's just something that has always been said, that was easily believed—about this warrior tribe who hunt with bows and arrows and wear long penis gourds and not much else.

Stories of cannibalism, like rape, weren't always connected to myths about barbarians, or even about monstrousness. Control of the processes of consumption confers great power, as we know from the priests officiating at the Christian mass. The faithful eat the body and drink the blood of Christ in the sacrament of the Eucharist, and this repeated miracle of transsubstantiation possibly meets a fundamental human desire to incorporate the object of passion, of wonder, of worship, of dread, of love. Every time a mother squeezes her child and murmurs, 'Mmm, you're so good I'm going to eat you', she's using the same imagery of union, of total commingling intimacy; every time lovers pretend to gnaw and bite each other, they're tapping the same metaphor. Oddly enough, the anticipation of cannibalism is naively self-flattering: my enemies want nothing better than to eat me, because I am so delicious. In these well-named acts of communion, a slippage occurs between actual and symbolic consumption of human flesh—and the arguments about the real presence of Jesus's body and blood have entangled further the confusion about the reality of cannibal acts.

Cannibalism isn't of course a peculiarly Christian theme; it's common in classical myth, where it's an activity of the gods, on the whole, like rape. Zeus, king of all the gods, survives only because his mother, Rhea, foils his father's plan to eat him, as he has eaten all his elder brothers and sisters. She wraps up a baby-shaped stone in swaddling bands and Cronus swallows it happily; Cronus had been told that one of his sons would supplant him, hence his desire to rid himself of them. But his method of doing so later casts him in the maternal part: for Zeus, when he grows up, gives his father a drug which makes him vomit up alive all the other children in his body. In this way, the famous Olympians—Hera, Demeter, Hades, Hestia, Poseidon—reenter the world, twice born of their father, begotten and brought forth. The devouring here acts as a prelude to birth; incorporation turns into a surrogate pregnancy.

The Greeks, it must be said, often felt awkward about the spectacular uncouthness of divine conduct. The poet Pindar, in his first Olympian ode, apologises for mythic extravagance, and then exclaims,

'Far be it from me to call any one of the blessed gods a cannibal!'

But he had to, as he went on to describe the feast at which the Titan Tantalus served up his son to see if the gods could tell the difference between roast animal and human flesh.

Cannibalism often occurs in myth alongside incest; both demonstrate the gods' outrageous flouting of human laws. Cronus commits one crime against human order by eating his children, and another because they're his by his sister Rhea. Later, Zeus and Hera as well as several other marriages and unions among the Olympians would continue the custom. Incest figures as a form of metaphorical cannibalism: eating your own. It also conveys a terrible incapacity to recognise your own: cannibals fail to see their prey as their kind, and this is an act which effectively exiles them from humanity. Both acts also relate to fears and longings in deeper ways: they offer an image of the transgressive acts of intimacy. In both, the perpetrator oversteps the bounds of kinship. When Princess Marie Bonaparte was considering incest with her son, she asked Freud, who was analysing her, his opinion, and he responded with a comparison to cannibalism: '[there are] no grounds whatever against eating human flesh instead of animal flesh. Still most of us would find it quite impossible . . . ' She seems to have agreed.

Cronus eats his own children and then gives birth to them: they are of his body and his blood in more ways than one. Incest at the start of time secures the resemblance of the species to its founding ancestors, it guarantees the purity of lineal descent. As the anthropologist Edmund Leach pointed out, original incest gives an imaginative reply to the vexing question, Where do we come from? If Adam and Eve's children didn't marry one another, they must have married someone else, and if they're the first and only humans, then they must have joined with non-humans. So, at the beginning, there's either incest, or mating with aliens. When the gods or mortals marry out of the human family the results are hybrids, monsters, beasts, creatures who are definitely not like us. In Genesis, too, there's an obscure passage about the daughters of men coupling with giants—and this heterodox mating becomes one of the reasons God opens the heavens to wash away human wickedness with the Flood.

Cannibalism is a key metaphor of outrageous transgression and its imagery traditionally conveys another—the crime of incest. This language recurs in medieval stories, like the romance of *Apollonius of Tyre,* one of the best-loved tales of the Middle Ages, extant in dozens of languages and manuscripts since the tenth century. The romance opens with a king and his daughter, the classic fairy-tale couple; only in this case, he won't relinquish his beloved princess but: 'Spurred on by the frenzy of his lust, he took his daughter's virginity by force, in spite of her lengthy resistance.' Afterwards, she wants to kill herself, but her nurse, like Juliet's, an unreliable counsellor, persuades her to resign herself to her lot and live as her father's secret concubine. Her father then wards off all suitors by setting an impossible enigma: if they can't solve it, they will die.

Shakespeare's late fairy-tale play, *Pericles,* was inspired by *Apollonius.* The riddle there is put to the hero:

I am no viper, yet I feed
On mother's flesh which did me breed.

It doesn't seem very tangled, and indeed, Apollonius guesses that the lovely girl is living in sinful union with her father. ' "Nor did you lie", he tells the king, "when you said, 'I eat my mother's flesh': Look to your daughter." '

Two elements in these instances of anthropophagy linger on in modern myths: the intrinsic, literal, gut (!) appeal of transgressive inversion, and the underlying connection with rampant and uncontrolled conduct, with men sleeping with their own offspring, like animals who know no better. Cannibalism combines so much possible lawlessness and irrationality that it communicates magical sovereignty in one of the forms which most continues to grip the human imagination. When the perpetrator isn't a god, eating human flesh becomes a distinguishing radical sign of the Beast—all devils are ravenous, and in Christian images of hell, covered in multiple orifices, busy gorging on themselves and one another.

Cannibalism, however, comes in four permutations, broadly speaking: raw or cooked, your own flesh or your enemies'. The Ogre in *Jack the Giant Killer,* like many other monsters of fairy tale, dines on human after the famous refrain,

Fee Fie Fo Fum
I smell the blood of an Englishman,
Be he alive or be he dead,
I'll grind his bones to make my bread.

He ends up tricked into eating his own children. Travelling back to England once, I was sitting next to a cheerful Cornishman; as we flew in over Devon, he remarked with a smile, 'Oh, you have to tread carefully with them, they eat their young down there.'

But the first image that springs to most people's minds when they hear the word cannibal isn't a Greek god or a fairy-tale villain or a Devon family. I was brought up for some of my childhood in Belgium, surrounded by images of their colony, the Congo, as Zaire was then known; among them many jokes about 'long pig', and much talk of missionaries trussed and spitted or standing in stewpots over cooking fires, as patient as early Christian martyrs in the arena. Some of this was facetious, but at the same time, it wasn't questioned—as it isn't in Evelyn Waugh's *Black Mischief*. Behind these preconceptions, lies a history.

In the age of the conquistadors, the word 'cannibal' was adopted from the people of 'Carib', in whom Columbus confidently recognised the famed anthropophagi, or man-eaters, of myth. Like the gold which he was certain was always round the next headland, it was always the tribe over the next ridge who were feasting on human flesh. Columbus left the myth of cannibalism thriving, but no account of the practice.

By the fifteenth century, the sign of being a barbarian, rather than an ogre, was a preference for cooked rather than raw human flesh. The word 'barbecue' is indeed one of the words, like 'hammock', borrowed into English from the language of the Taino people of the Americas. Though the Taino themselves were famed for their gentleness, the evolution of the word 'Carib' into cannibal conveys how Indians in that area came to be considered eaters of human flesh, never happy unless they were roasting the spiced joints of their victims on their ingenious grills over open fires. Shakespeare's 'savage and deformed slave', Caliban, in *The Tempest,* echoes this derivation.

Eyewitness accounts have proved highly elusive; believers in cannibalism taking the view that ipso facto nobody survived to tell the tale, sceptics arguing that the fantasy recurs in almost all people's insults against aliens: Christians were obvious candidates for the accusation during the Roman persecutions; later, in the Middle Ages, pogroms were unleashed against Jews charged with eating Christian children; the same outrage was considered routine among witches—they needed to render down baby fat to make their flying ointment. Only then could they take off on their broomsticks to the Sabbath. Thus one excessive fantasy becomes necessary to another in the mad but lucid circuitry of the imagination. In Australia, aborigines were credited with a particular taste for Chinese; rumours of their manhunts are still being repeated—with no evidence whatsoever. The gastronomy of cannibals—their culinary procedures and table manners—were similarly envisaged in precise detail, indeed, as precisely as the black masses of devil worshippers were rumoured to reproduce Christian solemnities in macabre inversion.

When the Dutch painter Albert Eckhout was commissioned to paint the flora and fauna and inhabitants of Brazil by the great soldier-prince Johan Mauritz of Nassau, he produced the most powerful extant early portraits of different tribespeople, men and women and children. In 1641, he painted a woman of the Tapuya tribe with a severed foot sticking out of the basket on her back, toying with a severed arm in her hand—but was he recording the evidence of his eyes? Had he observed her in the same way as he'd scanned the seedpods and knobbly rinds of the tropical fruits he painted for his patron? Flora are inevitably consenting subjects, but his living models, the Indians who appear in the magnificent life-size studies now in Copenhagen, may not have posed for the artist. He may have supplied features from his own presuppositions. Yet Eckhout even depicts a hunting party in the distance, actually positioned between the woman's parted legs, right under the apron of leaves she's wearing, while her hound laps at the ground between her feet baring its teeth—all this conveying barbarous appetites.

It would be silly to pretend that in the violence of conquest nobody was ever barbarically dismembered, or butchered or hideously dealt with after death; and there's evidence for ritual ingestion of human remains at funeral feasts as well as the obvious, bloodthirsty human sacrifices of the Aztecs. But empirical support for cannibalism as a routine form of sustenance has never been found; that it was a needed source of protein, as one historian even suggests, is simply fanciful. Yet the idea refuses to go away. A BBC series on the Empire included an introduction to the Caribbean which said, 'When the British first arrived . . . the necklace of lush tropical islands . . . was still largely the preserve of cannibals.' This was 1972! It's really only in the last decade that historical study has established how deeply fantasy shaped the story and the chronicles of conquest. Cannibalism helped to justify, of course, the presence of the invader, the settler, the trader, bringing civilisation. The centre has to draw outlines to give itself definition. The city has need of the barbarians to know what it is. The self needs the other to establish a sense of integral identity. If my enemies are like me, how can I go on feeling enmity against them?

Cannibalism marks its practitioners as throwbacks, barbarians, Stone Age men; yet the conqueror's imagery can betray that he is himself the devourer, like the slavers throwing overboard the dead and dying. Trophy-hunting isn't the province of savages: the cabinets of curiosities of the early modern connoisseur were filled with grisly spoils. The phrase 'I'll have your guts for garters' catches the universal impulse.

Cannibalism is used to define the alien but actually mirrors the speaker. By tarring the savage with the horror of cannibalism,

settlers, explorers, colonisers would vindicate their own violence—it's a psychological manoeuvre of great effectiveness.
Seeing the conquered as brute barbarians helped the confidence
of the first empire builders. Early on, however, there were dis-
senting voices. Montaigne, who had reminded his readers that
they were as savage as their victims, lamented the plundering of
the New World in a great threnody:

> . . . so many goodly citties ransacked and razed; so many
> nations destroyed and made desolate; so [many] infinite
> millions of harmlesse peoples of all sexes, stages and ages,
> massacred, ravaged and put to the sword; and the richest,
> the fairest and the best part of the world topsiturvied, ru-
> ined and defaced for the traffick in Pearles and Pepper. Oh
> mechanical victories, oh base conquest!

Montaigne's defence of the Indians seems to have affected
Shakespeare in *The Tempest*. The play was inspired by the mi-
raculous survival of a group of early colonists after a shipwreck
in the Caribbean, and Shakespeare follows reports of first con-
tacts when he describes how Caliban greets the mariners kindly
and helps them survive by gathering the unfamiliar food and
fishing for them. Like the Indians whom buccaneers treated
with—Roger North in Guyana and Walter Raleigh in Virginia—
Caliban shows the new arrivals, Prospero and his daughter, 'all
the qualities o' th' isle.' In spite of the overtones of Caliban's
name, Shakespeare doesn't represent his 'monster' as a consumer
of human flesh at all, but rather of 'pig-nuts' and 'filberts'. But
his portrait is ambiguous, as the amount and variety of stagings
and interpretations show. He does describe Caliban as 'savage',
'a freckled whelp, hag-born', who doesn't know language before

Prospero teaches him, and has since learnt only how to curse. Nevertheless, Caliban is given some of the most lyrical and anguished passages of poetry in the play.

This contradiction at the heart of the characterisation has turned Caliban into a mythic figure beyond the confines of *The Tempest* itself, and he has consequently become a key symbol in the discussion of colonialism, and its attendant ills, including racism.

Caliban has been played over the years as a kind of fish, or a manatee, as a wild man like Orson the bear cub, as a green man, a classical satyr, a half-naked Indian, or, as one actor's wife commented, 'half-monkey, half coconut'. In the postwar period, when the various empires were beginning to come to a kind of end, the figure of the dispossessed native slave inspires new interpretations—from Caliban's point of view. W. H. Auden, in 'The Sea and the Mirror' of 1944, glimpsed how Caliban might refuse to be the subject of his masters' serene providence, how the relations of dominance and economic power might crack. The colonial psychologist Octave Mannoni pioneered in 1950 the explicit interpretation of Caliban as a colonial subject, raging impotently against his oppression, unable to articulate his freedom or his rights, caught in a vicious spiral of powerlessness and petty retaliation. Roberto Fernández Retamar, in a subsequent impassioned essay, focussed on Caliban's blackness, and the poet Aimé Césaire, the longtime mayor of Fort-de-France in Martinique, gave a Marxist spin to this idea in 1960, with a rhapsodic, whirling version of *The Tempest* in which Caliban becomes a freedom fighter for the inhabitants of the island, and like a Toussaint l'Ouverture, rises against the coloniser, Prospero.

Caliban's role touches one of the most sensitive areas in contemporary race relations; he reveals once again how the perception of civilisation and barbarism so often turned on the question of alliance and family. The exchange between Prospero and Caliban, when Prospero gives the reasons for his rejection of Caliban, is highly revealing:

PROSPERO: I have us'd thee,
Filth as thou art, with human care;
 and lodg'd thee
In mine own cell, till thou didst seek to violate
The honour of my child . . .

CALIBAN: O ho, o ho! woulds't it had been done!
Thou didst prevent me; I had peopled else
This isle with Calibans.

So, Caliban's segregation as a monster beyond the pale takes place only after he's tried to violate Miranda. Before that, he had lived with them as if he were one of the family. But one rape could hardly have engendered a population for the island—these lines express those old fears of heterodox misalliance. They also hint at a kind of incest between Caliban, Prospero's foster child, and Miranda, Prospero's daughter. There's even a hint that Prospero may be more than a foster father when he says of Caliban, at the end, 'This thing of darkness I acknowledge mine'. Caliban's threat conveys the fear of hybridisation: the monster might produce monstrous progeny.

These same fantasies continue in popular attitudes to black immigration and to intermarriage between races: in the film of *King Kong*, for instance, Kong is represented as both cannibal and rapist, and Fay Wray, the Miranda figure, has to be defended from him so that she can be properly bestowed on a Ferdinand-like juvenile lead. Caliban's threat of proliferation continues to resonate: when people are asked to give the size of the black population in Britain, they sometimes put it as high as a quarter of the total. The real figure is around a twentieth. The Runnymede Trust in 1991 conducted a survey and found that more than 90 per cent made wildly exaggerated guesses.

The Tempest concludes with the restoration of harmony, the obedient love of Miranda and Ferdinand, and Caliban's promise that he'll 'be wise hereafter and sue for grace'—a reference to his possible baptism. It's interesting to note that in 1611, that is around the time Shakespeare was writing the play, the son of a prince from Guinea called Caddi-biah—another echo of the name Caliban—was christened in the church of St Mildred Poultry in the City of London, the very quarter where stood the Rose and the Globe theatres and the inns Shakespeare frequented. The boy had been entrusted to one John Davies, of the English ship the *Abigail,* by his father. Or so the register related. Even if the coincidence of the name Caddi-biah is meaningless, the presence of the Christian, African youth in London upsets received ideas about the history of migration; it puts paid to the prevalent opinion that black people only arrived in Britain with the waves of workers invited after the war. There are entries in parish registers from the seventeenth century of births and deaths of children born to English and African couples; while, abroad, in the new possessions, intermarriage was far more common than has been admitted. Not all converted, however: the brother-in-law of the famous princess of the Algonquin tribe, Pocahontas, for example, refused to be baptised, preferring—one contemporary reported, 'to sing and dance his diabolicall measures'.

The Church of St Mildred Poultry has vanished: only office

buildings, gleaming in glass and steel, now rise around the area. The disappearance of so many of the old City buildings has been followed by the disappearance of most of the residents. This scattering in itself has carried off the memory of an earlier time— including the recollection of the earliest black Englishmen and women. Memory is made of tough shiny stuff, which won't absorb new imprints. It's perhaps relevant that the 1993 England football team, with its black captain, Paul Ince, and other black players, are all represented white in the table version of the game Subbuteo. Yet far less historically attested tales cling on, about cannibals practising savage rites in some distant place.

In this context, it's interesting to discover that the Mandingo, a people of Guinea, ascribe the birth of narrative itself to cannibalism. But in this story, cannibalism is an act of a rather different order to the crimes in Western storytelling: a man dying of hunger tells the friend with whom he's travelling that he can go no further. His friend tells him to wait, and he'll bring him something to eat. He disappears, and soon returns with a steaming dish which saves the dying man's life. Many years later— the traditional storyteller would spin out this interval—seven years, seven months, seven weeks later, when they meet again, the good samaritan reveals that he hadn't shot a deer, or a bird, or even an elephant for his dying friend those many long years ago, No, he had cut the flesh from his own thigh and cooked it. When the recipient hears this, he replies, 'The memory of your kindness will never be lost, I will tell this story to sing your praises all my life, and pass it on to my descendants, and they will continue.' In this way, the *griot,* the storyteller of West African society, came about. The tale, told today by the French writer Tierno Monénembo, originally from Guinea, also wittily inverts the usual Western attitudes to barbarians—the act seen as defining their brutal inhumanity becomes proof instead of an excessive altruism.

Cannibalism has taken place and has been—and is—very widely and deeply experienced—in the imagination. It has been practised, in my view, very rarely and in extremis by individuals. But the fantasy lay on the surface of the minds of the explorers from Europe, from centuries of myth-taking, an expression of deep desires and passions and terrors, when they reached those places they called the Indies. And it has survived and still influences attitudes today.

That imagery of forbidden ingestion masked other powerful longings and fears—about mingling and hybridity, about losing definition, about swallowing and being swallowed—fears about a future loss of identity, about the changes that history itself brings.

But new voices are being raised to confront this legacy. The terrible story which inspired Turner to paint 'The Slave Ship' has continued to resonate: it has that extreme, cautionary quality of myth. Barry Unsworth in his novel *Sacred Hunger* developed the *Zong*'s crime, and the Guyanese-born poet David Dabydeen has written a long lyric sequence, called 'Turner', which, unlike the artist, unlike Ruskin, gives a voice to one of the drowned slaves in the painting and imagines the atrocity from his point of view. The drowned slave struggles to dream of the future he has lost but still wants to make but his memories oppress him:

> *no noise*
> *Comes from my mouth, no lamentation*
> *As I fall towards the sea, my breath held*
> *In shock until the waters quell me.*

Struggle came only after death, the flush
Of betrayal, and hate hardening my body
Like cork, buoying me when I should have sunk . . .
To these depths . . .
         where the sea, with an undertaker's
Touch, soothes and erases pain from the faces
Of drowned sailors, unpastes flesh from bone
With all its scars, boils, stubble, marks
Of debauchery. . . .
I wanted to begin anew in the sea
But . . .
        my face was rooted
In the ground of memory, a ground stampeded
By herds of foreign men who swallow all its fruit
And leave a trail of dung for flies
To colonize; a tongueless earth, bereft
Of song except for the idiot witter
Of wind through a dead wood.

Dabydeen is using his poem to repair that loss, he's putting his song in the place of his subject's imposed silence. From submersion, from engulfment, the images can return, the drowned can rise, the devoured be pierced together and the cannibalised past be heard, telling its stories.

SIX

HOME

Our Famous Island Race

In the cabinet War Rooms, an austere, utility-furnished warren of basement offices in Whitehall, where, as the brochure says, 'everything is absolutely authentic', you can still see Churchill's high, lumpy, single bed. There's a battery of turquoise, scarlet and cream Bakelite telephones on view, one or two skimpy electric bar fires and lots of very ample ashtrays. Strategic maps—of The World, of The British Empire—unfurl on the walls, with lines of coloured wool indicating the position of the armies—red for the British front line, black for the German, blue for the Free French, mauve for Vichy. Invasion is the issue, and this modest basement was the nerve centre of the resistance.

The Rooms were opened to the public by the Prime Minister, Margaret Thatcher, in the spring of 1984, not long after the victory in the Falklands; they're a monument to one moment of defining national identity, opened to the public at another. Here, Churchill's rousing calls, broadcast from these rooms in September 1940, are replayed to the visitor: 'These cruel, wanton, indiscriminate bombings are of course part of Hitler's invasion plan. He hopes, by killing large numbers of civilians, and women and children, that he will terrorise and cow the people of this mighty imperial city. Little does he know the spirit of the British nation. This wicked man has now resolved to break our famous island race . . .'

Churchill makes his appeal to the British as members of an island race. But significantly, the evidence of the maps hanging on the walls around give the lie to the image of the isolated sceptred isle, the little world all on its own. They make it clear that the nation could only survive, be victualled, watered, armed, supplied through connection across borders, through the convoys which set out from the ports and entrepots of the empire, its allies and sympathisers. Here they are, marked on the map—Kingston, Jamaica; Port of Spain, Trinidad; Aruba, Curaçao, Bermuda, Puerto Rico, Recife, Halifax, St John's, Sydney, Gibraltar, Oran, Algiers, Casablanca, the Azores, Dakar, Bathurst, Freetown, Reykjavik, and many others. Other islands, a constellation of islands, other harbours, a star map of interconnection, a necklace of many stones set in as many seas, the collaboration of many peoples and places and ports—the antithesis of self-sufficiency in isolation.

The myth of national identity desires to forget this historical contingency, this interrelatedness. As a national hero, Churchill still has no rival, as Mrs Thatcher knew, when she purposefully placed herself in his long shadow. In her memoirs, she remarks, with disingenuous cosiness, 'I am glad that Chequers played a large part in the Falklands story. Churchill had used it quite a lot during the Second World War and its atmosphere helped to get us all together.' Throughout, she stresses that the Falklanders are 'an island race, like the people of the United Kingdom', and she winds up her account with her speech at Cheltenham, harking back: 'We rejoice that Britain has rekindled that spirit which has fired her for generations past . . .'

The idea of return to an ancient national insularity also turned up in Michael Portillo's recent bark from the moral high ground: 'Britain has been unusually fortunate,' he declared, 'in that as an island nation we have for centuries rarely had to think about how we define ourselves'. But it was now time, he went on, 'to temper our traditional tolerance'. It's interesting that Portillo himself has benefited from that traditional tolerance, as the son of a Spaniard on the Republican side in the Civil War, who must have preferred England to the intolerance of fascism.

In a dreamier vein, John Major earlier also resisted encroachment from abroad, from the Continent, evoking a permanent, unchanging national idyll in his famous speech to the Conservative Europe group in the Mansion House, in April 1993. The Prime Minister invoked 'a country of long shadows on county grounds, warm beer, invincible green suburbs, dog lovers—and as George Orwell said, "old maids bicycling to Holy Communion through the morning mist . . . " Britain,' the Prime Minister promised, 'will survive unamendable in all essentials . . .'

Orwell was writing in 1941, and it doesn't really need me to say that all these essentials have been through some amendments—not least that old maids might be bicycling to church to administer the sacrament as priests. The nostalgic strain of the British temper was already parodied, with cool irony, by W. H. Auden in 'The Sea and the Mirror'. There, Caliban imagines a colonial servant, adrift among imperial possessions, yearning to return:

> Carry me back, Master, to the cathedral town where the canons run through the water meadows with butterfly nets and the old women keep sweetshops in the cobbled side streets, or back to the upland mill town (gunpowder and plush) with its grope-movie and its pool-room lit by gas, carry me back to the days before my wife had put on weight, back to the years when the beer was cheap and the rivers really froze in winter . . . Give me my passage home . . .

Home takes us back to a golden afternoon in the past, and this brings in the question of memory, which in turn raises history as an issue. Voltaire's justly famous epigram declares that history is 'une fable convenue', an agreed fable: contemporary nationalisms press agreement to their version; this is why history has become such an acute, immediate issue, why members of a democracy which wishes to survive have to take part in the telling of the story, examine and resist the self-serving fables of political ambitions. In the new states of former Yugoslavia and the Soviet Union, old city names and old street names have returned, monuments have been defaced and old ones freshly reinstated. In Zagreb the square of the 'Victims of Fascism' has been renamed the Square of the 'Croatian Kings'; old tsars and old tyrants are being recovered from the annals; in Italy, Alessandra Mussolini, the granddaughter of the dictator, is even able to trade on the family name.

Arguing with the past, like paying taxes, like observing the law, like queueing, like not playing music full blast when others will be disturbed, has suddenly become a vital part of being a member of society, an ordinary but important act of citizenship, a factor in establishing the idea of home as a place you would like to belong, and might be allowed to stay. With the upheavals in Eastern Europe, Western Europe begins to stir too, and different fundamentalisms have discovered the power of historical arguments to shape their reality. The British, floundering after years of authority abroad, fear loss of self when the story's changing—rising nationalists of different stripes finger different culprits: Europe, former Commonwealth citizens, new immigrants from the former eastern bloc and elsewhere. And the hunger for the ascertainable, unamendable homeland turns dangerous.

While European nations struggle increasingly to define their difference from one another, another population has grown in numbers in their midst. For thousands, home has become a mythical lost continent, visible under the flux, but harder than ever to reach. The UN Council for Refugees can't even estimate how many millions of people are on the move, or will be in coming years, as new borders are being drawn on the map, year by year, sometimes week by week. Like a forest fire, they drive people into flight as they advance. Never have there been so many newly patrolled territories, keeping one lot in and another lot out. Not since the huge emigrations of 1890–1924 have so many people looked for work in other countries: Italy, Spain, and Greece, according to one report, may have a million illegal residents. In San Francisco, recently, I asked a taxi driver where he was from. 'I'm an illegal,' he replied, without hesitation, as if it were a well established nationality in itself. Homelessness meanwhile has become the predicament of our time.

In France, the homeless are called 'les sans-abri', the shelterless ones. Some of the earliest writing in the world represents a roof, an inverted V on two poles, the same cipher for home children draw in their first scribbles, alongside the stick figures of family and self. But home, in English, also encloses the idea of *patria*, which in French or Italian is conveyed as 'pays' and 'paese', words distinct from 'ma maison' or 'casa mia', and this theme lies even more acutely at the core of contemporary concerns. Home meant native land to the earliest homeward voyager—Odysseus, the emblematic figure of the century not only for James Joyce but for Derek Walcott, too, the great contemporary interpreter of ideas about home and homing who has written his own odyssey in the book-length poem 'Omeros'. For Homer's Odysseus, home simply meant Ithaca, the land he owned and governed, too: home as property and place of authority. His patrimony, inherited from his father and guarded by his wife, Penelope, in his long absence, is symbolised in Homer by Odysseus's marital bed, which he himself built around an olive tree still living, still rooted in the soil of his island.

The question of home's so simple in the *Odyssey*. Odysseus earns his return through suffering and perseverance—and fidelity throughout to his goddess Athena and—in spirit at least—to his wife, Penelope. But home ownership, that flag of Toryism, can't be translated into home in the larger sense any longer; some people may indeed have assembled their own bed from a do-it-yourself kit under their own roof in the country where they were born. But not even this assures them that they are home. Second, third, fourth generation peoples born in the US or in the UK feel themselves part of what Salman Rushdie has called, in a memorable phrase, 'imaginary homelands', countries of the mind, of memory, of history, of faith and increasingly of racial species and micro-species—nations composed of hankerings and loss, of a utopian nostalgia. Many of these self-banished, cosmopolitan communities live in an existential dislocation, even if they themselves haven't been moved.

The struggle for the story of the past sets markers on the map of the present which in turn chart the future. But memory leads down many roads: to triumphalism, on the one hand, to grudge on the other, as well as to discovery and reparation. Roots revivalism—the politics of nostalgia—can lead to reinvigorated pride among muffled or neglected peoples or groups: but remembering sufferings like the loss of home can also be made a pretext for vengeance in the present.

Increasingly, the old ideas of assimilation in an adopted country are being overtaken by different thinking on identity and belonging, by a new mythology of home, as somewhere else to which attachment is felt, by blood, by religion, by language, or even, by elective affinity—by choice. If those idealistic reasons for which the last war against fascism was fought—by all those various allies—are to be honoured at all, it seems to me vital that a common culture of citizenship, based on shared principles of justice, argued out between equals with equal voices, is helped to develop and grow and make a new homeland.

Growing ethnic hatreds between peoples who share the same streets and closely resemble one another argue their cause from historical wrongs: memory and imagination pitch in to tell their stories in the contest for borders, for dominion, and for righteousness. Monsters breed in this terrible playground of fabricated identity, and all the hostile stratagems of labelling and differentiation I've tried to describe in the earlier lectures press for vindication of us against them, of self against other, of Loyalist against Republican, Chetnik against Ustashe, Arab against Jew, England against Brussels and Strasbourg. One group will insist on its title to its home in certain, inhospitable terms, which can turn a lifelong neighbour into a hostile stranger overnight, a casual community into an embattled tribe and locate cannibals in the back garden and chimaeras under the bed. At the core of the struggle for home lies the struggle for the way the story of place is told. Between what is remembered and what is forgotten, the self takes its bearings for home. The question is no longer who is to guard the guardians, but who's to tell the story? Who can bear witness?

At the heart of Romantic nationalism lies the interdependency of home, ethnic identity, heritage, and women—and this mythology of the hearth continues to flourish in the present nationalist revival.

The Grimm brothers, living at a time of Germany's struggles against Napoleonic occupation, belonged to the literary and scholarly circles determined to maintain and foster and define their national culture in the face of the invader; they became passionate about stories told by ordinary people, which had previously been scorned as mere old wives' tales, as the nonsensical wishful thinking of the illiterate, coarse and foolish romancing. The Grimms began to collect them for their famous anthology, which first appeared in 1812. The stories were seen as authentic and archaic, flowing from the streams of the forests, falling with the needles of the pine trees: the brothers exulted over the word-perfect repetition of some of their sources because this seemed evidence of the stories' immemorial antiquity, of an unbroken, homegrown tradition. They did notice, however, that one or two rather resembled the fairy tales in Charles Perrault's famous French collection of over a century earlier, and that yet others echoed Italian ones of even earlier date, and in some instances, they dropped these inauthentic, impure, non-German stories. It's only today, after much scholarly research into fairy tales, that it has become plain that the brothers' sources were saturated in the French tradition, which itself goes back to the Italian, and the Arabian, and the Indian, and the Chinese, and so forth—of all branches of literature, fairy tales offer the strongest evidence of bonds in common across borders of nations, race and language. A heroine with a very small foot, on her way to a feast dressed in a cloak of kingfisher feathers produced for her by magic, loses her slipper in a Chinese fairy tale written down in the ninth century; and the first beast bridegroom who appears only by night slips into his mortal beloved's bed in an Indian story of two thousand years ago.

The hearthside crone who passes on the wisdom of the tribe, who epitomises the once upon a time when all was well, has always been a polyglot cosmopolitan, in spite of her homely head shawl and those old, regional clogs she wears and her funny beaked nose and her spinning wheel. Her oral tradition, too, has been mixed and brewed and peppered and spiced with much written, literary material from all kinds of heterogeneous origins—the transmission of myths and romances, fables and proverbs took multiple pathways, as it still does today. This motley, mongrel, volatile character of folklore is of crucial importance, because even while stories are patently connected to particular places and peoples, as in the case of Hindu epics or the Irish legends, they aren't immutable. They're not even recuperable in some imagined integrity, because the act of recuperation itself and the context of the retelling affect the interpretation. The primordial past, in all its longed-for simplicity and purity, can't lie hidden inside them like perfume still smelling in some pharaoh's tomb. Home lies ahead, in the unfolding of the story in the future, not behind waiting to be regained.

This romantic figment of the folk hearth returns us once more to mum, she who embodies birthplace as well as the larger allegories of native land, and by extension of nation. But she can only fulfil this role at the price of shedding personal history, of claiming timelessness and unchangingness. Home in myth promises an end to questing, to wandering, to trouble—home is closure, the arrival brings the story to an end, with all the wicked suitors dead, the faithful dog happy in his last breath, and your wife still staunch and true at her pious task of weaving your father's shroud. Your return signals your escape from misadventures, the great public events of your career—in a sense you can now shut the door on history. Among the Phaeacians, in the palace of Alcinous and Arete, Odysseus asks the minstrel Demodocus to sing once again about the Trojan War and his own exploits, and as he listens, he weeps for pity. All of that lies behind him: the home where he is headed is a place where history lies behind you. The domestic hearth, coded female, burns to the side of the great events with which the returning hero busied himself.

The effect is that home does not figure at the centre of the story, nor as a product of enterprise, as the sum of the work of its members, as evolving—earned even—through men and women's labour together. In this, Odysseus, the Greek wanderer of myth, anticipates the fracture between home and factory of the industrial revolution, and the present separation between the woman's realm and the man's, women's control of household and children, men's work and street life, with occasional homings—to Mum with the laundry, to the wife, or the girlfriend, with a bottle by way of apology. This myth disconnects home from work, makes women's tasks seem natural, timeless, somehow inevitable; it contributes to the continuing inability of our society to appreciate that raising a family and making a home is labour, as intricately bound up with economic conditions as any other kind of work.

The association of the primordial, static, authentic origin with the feminine realm runs deep in national myths, in this country, and perhaps in all of former Christendom where the Virgin Mary and her child symbolised an unsullied state of humanity and promised redemption. But England was 'Our Lady's dower', and Marian devotion flung a blue mantle of churches dedicated to her over the whole country until the Reformation. Her symbolic function then passed to queens, beginning with Gloriana or Astraea, Elizabeth I, and culminating in the present trinity of Queen Mother, Queen, and Princess Diana.

An exemplary exhibition at the National Gallery, London, recently interpreted the exquisite anonymous Wilton Diptych, painted around 1395. Richard II, kneeling to the Virgin in the Wilton Diptych, accompanied by two of England's sainted kings—Edward the Confessor and Edmund—offers an image of a new adoration of the kings, with three English monarchs in the place of the Magi, and their offering, perhaps, the country itself, whose banner, blazoned with the red cross of St George, is being held by one of the company of angels who surround the Virgin, and who wear the livery badge of the king himself, the White Hart. The banner's staff is surmounted by a tiny globe in which the tiny world, the sceptred isle has been painted in miniature.

This icon, which gives every apparent sign of profound spirituality, in fact contains powerful partisan arguments about king and country. Richard II himself was a prime mover in fostering the concept of a sacred monarchy: he laid down the rules for royal coronations and funerals, he commissioned hieratic portraits of himself, and he promoted with his own assiduous attentions the cult of Westminster Abbey's buried kings, beside whom he wanted to lie himself. But what is highly significant, from the point of view of modern ideas of national identity, is that when Richard II is shown extending his royal court to include heaven and the heavenly host, he's also yielding himself to a paradise of women, presided over by the Virgin. Her attendant, androgynous angels with their long golden ringlets, chaplets of roses, tiny rosebud mouths in pink, and white beardless faces wear blue gowns in honour of the Madonna.

The makers of the Wilton Diptych were arguing with history—they may have even been arguing with the past, as Richard, portrayed in the image as a youth, at the time of his coronation, may have already been murdered when it was painted; so it may be a votive image, created by his supporters after his cousin Bolingbroke seized the throne and became Henry IV. The icon's royalism, in its delicacy and sense of the sacred, would seem to have little in common with our contemporary monarchy, with Charles and Di, or Prince Philip and the Queen and the shouting headlines, the dirty tricks, the squalid eavesdropping. But they are still connected. In several respects, the Wilton Diptych conveys an enduring and vital idea of the imaginary homeland— which the royal family is still expected to embody. Much of the present disgust with them isn't rooted in a republican philosophy but in a nostalgic royalist idealism.

Richard descends from a line of kings, the imagery makes clear, he belongs in an unbroken continuum of sanctity; the temporal character of his kingdom doesn't mean that it'll come to an end—it's been entrusted to the spiritual, eternal dimension warranted by the Virgin and her angels. Ancient, holy and enduring—Shakespeare enshrined this idea in many plays about kingship and England, but most of all in *Richard II*, in John of

Gaunt's ringing anthem. Here, in the famous sceptred isle speech, the metaphors of heaven, island, fortress, and house follow one upon the other as if by force or logic:

> This royal throne of kings, this scepter'd isle,
> This earth of majesty, this seat of Mars,
> This other Eden, demi-paradise,
> This fortress built by Nature for herself
> Against infection and the hand of war,
> This happy breed of men, this little world,
> This precious stone set in the silver sea,
> Which serves it in the office of a wall,
> Or as a moat defensive to a house,
> Against the envy of less happier lands,
> This blessed plot, this earth, this realm, this England . . .

And these images again turn back on themselves to invoke natural, bodily origin, land as mother:

> This nurse, this teeming womb of royal kings . . .
> this dear, dear, land . . .

The Virgin's former dower, the enclosed and impregnable isle: aspects of the mystic kingdom present in Richard II's icon, and repeated in Shakespeare's rhetoric. Yet, at the very same time, the painting's imagery contradicts the insularity of its message. The iconography of the Wilton Dipytch, for all its ideological patriotism, draws on the Catholic Church's Latin culture, jumping geographical borders, ignoring blood ties; the symbol of Richard's livery shows pods of broom, the *planta genista* of the Plantagenet dynasty, which was shared with England's long enemies, the French kings; the artist himself might have been a foreigner, and certainly a travelled man, as experts can tell from the techniques he used. Without these international, cultural means of expression, the diptych would be meaningless.

Nativism in splendid solitude can't be achieved at all, any more than a fairy tale can be purely homegrown.

The monarchy's symbolic role in the country's sense of identity has grown as its political power has withered. Present public anger with the royal family hasn't focussed on constitutional flaws, or on the social damage of aristocratic privilege, but has concentrated on their behaviour—they're betraying the monarchy's mystique, the ideal of royal Britain, defiling the chrism and the orb, the abbey and the palace, the coach and twelve, the colour trooped, all the glittering paraphernalia the tourist boards have presented as the nation since the invention of colour photography. The personal conduct of the royal family, since Victoria's reign, has been expected to offer the domestic version of this sanctity, the hearthside story of national identity—with a certain class colouring, of course. The Queen and her mother also distilled a familiar essence of Britain—with their horses and corgies, malvern water and Earl Grey tea, cardigans, brogues, silver-framed photographs, jigsaw puzzles and the wireless, their weak and not entirely reliable menfolk. That catchphrase, 'so very different from the home life of our own dear Queen', used to characterise anything untoward, was first spoken in Victoria's reign, and still conveys the extent to which the Queen symbolises the imaginary personality of the nation. So it's striking that the Windsor Castle fire did not much stir her subjects' sympathy— only £25,000 was sent towards the £40 million needed for the repair fund; to make up the deficit, Buckingham Palace was opened to the public for the first time. The Queen thus resorted to putting one home on show in order to restore another; but popular indifference revealed that her country house burning down was perceived as fitting punishment for her family's failing to keep faith with the national ideal of home. The same matriarchal atavism runs down through to the conservatives' belief in the traditional role of the mother in the home; even while their economic policies make it impossible.

Diana's perfections appeared at first fully warranted by the widespread trust in her virginity. The mythic tenacity of this image of the symbolic female nation is so great that it's making it hard for the British people to let go of Diana: she will be crowned queen, promised the Prime Minister, even though she'd be living apart from the king. It would be interesting to see the answer to a poll asking the public to choose between Charles for King on his own, or Diana as Queen Regent until William grows up.

Could there be another way of talking about home, without harking back to nostalgic lies about the hearth, the throne, the greensward, the island race? What is home ground? And how can it be made—now, for today?

Derek Walcott was given the Nobel Prize for literature in 1992. He was born in St Lucia when it was a British colony, and has inherited through his grandparents—both black and white— a double uprootedness: on one side transportations of black slaves from coastal West Africa to work sugar in the British West Indies, on the other, the displacement of those colonists who, to serve the empire, left home, as England was always known, however long those colonial families of empire had been gone. In his poetry and drama, Walcott has worked back and forth over the relations of home and history—like the swooping swifts of the Caribbean—which he describes plying in ceaseless motion over the sea. His work puts the dominant and anguished questions of this end of the millennium: what does it mean to belong and not to belong? What way can history be told and experience be lived to bring about a sense of belonging? How does one come home?

Over the last twenty years of writing, Walcott has struggled with the Odyssean idea of home as native place, with the yearning to return to origins, and speak out against the nationalisms that assault communities and their peace, against xenophobia. As Walcott declares, 'I bear/my house inside me, everywhere'.

The imaginary homeland is itself homeless. There's no home except in the mind, where ideas of home are grown—'I had no nation now, but the imagination,' he writes. Roots push down from ideas, from the internal maps held in each individual. Literature, the relating of history, the development of thought, access to and sharing of knowledge, the arts—including of course architecture, the act of building itself—all nourish this growth. It's vital not to abdicate from the making of this internal dwelling place. For stories held in common make and remake the world we inhabit. Walcott reproduces the dense mesh of modern identity, with its multiple compass points, its layered experiences; he stands witness to a rich—and painful—story made in common by both invader and invaded, coloniser and colonised, migrants and residents, crossing over all moats and fortress walls, navigating the oceans, like the convoys on the map in the cabinet War Rooms.

In a lyric poem of 1979, 'The Schooner Flight', the narrator leaves his home, breaks with his past, his roots, and ships as a seaman on board the schooner called *Flight*:

Though my Flight *never pass the incoming tide*
of this inland sea beyond the loud reefs
of the final Bahamas, I am satisfied
if my hand gave voice to one people's grief.
Open the map. More islands there, man,
than peas on a tin plate, all different size,
one thousand in the Bahamas alone,
from mountains to low scrub with coral keys,
and from this bowsprit, I bless every town,
the blue smell of smoke in hills behind them,
and the one small road winding down them like twine
to the roofs below; I have only one theme:
The bowsprit, the arrow, the longing, the lunging heart—
the flight to a target whose aim we'll never know,
vain search for one island that heals with its harbour
and a guiltless horizon, where the almond's shadow
doesn't injure the sand. There are so many islands!
As many islands as the stars at night
on that branched tree from which meteors are shaken
like falling fruit around the schooner Flight.

There's no safe place from the injuries of history; home as a place or a time of innocence can only be an illusion. But the poet doesn't recover the bitter past to serve present grudges—his acts of remembering, his quest for identity are grounded in generosity.

And from this sense at once of loss and recovery, this mix and merging, this reckoning with the complexities of the past, present national identity and patterns of belonging can be fruitfully formed. The way Walcott has worked the material of his complicated memories and inheritance in the Caribbean represents an exemplary openness to making a new model of the homeland, which doesn't exclude, but rather includes, which doesn't justify, but seeks to understand. No home is an island; no homegrown culture can thrive in permanent quarantine. We're all wayfarers and we make our destinations as we go.

The modern myths I've looked at in these lectures—monstrous mothers, warrior heroes, diabolical innocents, wild beasts and savage strangers—all belong in the larger story of home, which is still being told; they're all threaded through the fabric as it's being made. In Derek Walcott's stage version of *The Odyssey,* Menelaus, King of Sparta, declares, 'We earn home, like everything else.' Walcott doesn't mean paying the rent or the mortgage. He means taking part in the journey, using memory, imagination, and language to question, to remember and to repair, to wish things well without sentimentality, without rancour, always resisting the sweet seduction of despair.

BACKGROUND READING AND SOURCES

Amnesty International. *Women in the Front Line* (London, 1991)

Antoninus Liberalis. *The Metamorphoses.* Ed. & trans. Francis Celoria. (London, 1992)

Barthes, Roland. *Mythologies.* Trans. Annette Lavers. (New York, 1972)

Baudrillard, Jean. *The Transparency of Evil: Essays on Extreme Phenomena.* Trans. James Benedict. (London, 1993)

Blonsky, Marshall. *American Mythologies* (New York, 1992)

Bynum, Caroline Walker. *Fragmentation and Redemption: Essays on Gender and the Human Body in Medieval Religion* (New York, 1991)

Calasso, Roberto. *The Marriage of Cadmus & Harmony*. Trans. Tim Parks. (New York, 1993)

Cohen, Ruth; Loxall, Jill; Craig, Gary & Sadiq-Sangster, Azra. *Hardship Britain: Being Poor in the 1990s* (London, 1992)

Crary, Jonathan & Kwinter, Sanford. Eds. *Incorporations* (New York, 1992)

Davenport, Guy. *The Geography of the Imagination* (New York, 1983)

Detienne, Marcel. *The Gardens of Adonis: Spices in Greek Mythology*. Trans. Janet Lloyd. (Brighton, 1977)

Edmunds, Lowell. Ed. *Approaches to Greek Myth* (Baltimore, 1989)

Foucault, Michel. *The History of Sexuality: an Introduction*. Trans. Robert Hurley. (London, 1984)

Freedberg, David. *The Power of Images: Studies in the History and Theory of Response* (Chicago & London, 1989)

Fussell, Paul. *Bad. Or the Dumbing of America* (New York, 1991)

Griffin, Susan. *A Chorus of Stones: the Private Life of War* (New York, 1992)

Hamilton, Roberta & Barrett, Michèle. Eds. *The Politics of Diversity* (London, 1986)

Hillis Miller, J. *Illustration* (Berkeley, 1992)

Hobsbawm, Eric & Ranger, Terence. *The Invention of Tradition* (Cambridge, 1984)

Kirk, G. S. *The Nature of Greek Myths* (New York, 1983)

Namjoshi, Suniti. *St. Suniti and the Dragon* (London, 1994)

Nandy, Ashis. *At the Edge of Psychology: Essays in Politics and Culture* (Delhi & Oxford, 1990)

———. *Science, Hegemony and Violence: a Requiem for Modernity* (Oxford & New York, 1990)

————. *The Intimate Enemy: Loss and Recovery of Self Under Colonialism* (Oxford & New York, 1992)

————. *Traditions, Tyranny and Utopias: Essays in the Politics of the Awareness* (Delhi & Oxford, 1987)

Ovid. *Metamorphoses*. Trans. Mary Innes. (New York, 1973)

Paulin, Tom. *Minotaur: Poetry and the Nation State* (Cambridge, Mass., 1992)

Ricoeur, Paul. *Oneself as Another*. Trans. Kathleen Blamey. (Chicago, 1992)

Said, Edward. *Culture and Imperialism* (New York, 1993)

Sen, Amartya. 'On The Darwinian View of Progress', *London Review of Books*, 5 November 1992, pp. 15–19

Showalter, Elaine. *Sexual Anarchy: Gender and Culture at the Fin de Siècle* (New York, 1991)

Ugrěsič, Dubravka. *American Fictionary*. Trans. Celia Hawkesworth. (Evanston, forthcoming)

Vernant, Jean-Pierre. *Myth and Society in Ancient Greece*. Trans. Janet Lloyd. (New York, 1988)

————. *Religions, Histoires, Raisons* (Paris, 1979)

ONE

Apollonius of Rhodes. *The Voyage of Argo*. Trans. E. V. Rieu. (Cambridge, Mass., 1971)

Altaio, Vicenç & Veiga, Anna. Eds. *In Vitro De les Mitologies de la Fertilitat a las Limits de la Ciència* (Barcelona, 1992)

Bompiani, Ginerva. 'The Chimera Herself', in *Fragments for a History of the Human Body*. Eds. M. Feher, R. Naddaff, & N. Tazi. *Zone* 1, New York, 1989, pp. 365–409

Chapman, Allan. 'The Canon, the Chemist, and the Dinosaurs',

Oxford Today, Vol. 6, No. 1, pp. 25–7, Michaelmas 1993

Coomaraswamy. 'On the Loathly Bride', in *Selected Papers: Traditional Art and Symbolism.* Ed. Roger Lipsey. (Princeton, 1977)

Crichton, Michael. *Jurassic Park* (New York, 1990)

Dormor, Duncan J. *The Relationship Revolution: Cohabitation, Marriage, and Divorce in Contemporary Europe* (London, 1992)

Gibson, Pamela Church & Gibson, Roma. Eds. *Dirty Looks: Women, Pornography, Power* (London, 1993)

Gould, John. 'Law, Custom and Myth: Aspects of the Social Position of Women in Classical Athens', *Journal of the Historical Society,* 100, 1980, pp. 38–59

Gould, Stephen Jay. 'Dinomania', *New York Review of Books,* 12 August 1993, pp. 51–6

Husain, Shakrukh. Ed. *The Virago Book of Witches* (London, 1993)

Johnson, Judith. 'Women and Vampires: Nightmare or Utopia', *The Kenyon Review,* Vol. 5, No. 1, 1993, pp. 72–80

Keats, John. *The Complete Poems.* Ed. John Barnard. (New York, 1975)

Macaskill, Hilary. *From the Workhouse to the Workplace: 75 Years of One Parent Family Life* (London, 1993)

McNeil, Gil. Ed. *Soul Providers: Writings by Single Parents* (London, 1994)

National Council for One Parent Families. *Annual Report* (London, 1993)

Ovid. *Ovid's Heroines.* Trans. Daryl Hine. (New Haven & London, 1991)

Padel, Ruth. *In and Out of the Mind: Greek Images of the Tragic Self* (Princeton, 1992)

Parker, Hermione. *Citizen's Income and Women* (London, 1993)

Pembroke, Simon. 'Women in Charge: the Function of Alternatives in Early Greek Tradition and the Ancient Idea of Matriarchy', *Journal of the Warburg & Courtauld Institutes,* Vol. 30, 1967, pp. 1–36

Pizan, Christine de. *The Book of the City of Ladies*. Trans. Earl Jeffrey Richards. (New York, 1982)

Plath, Sylvia. *Ariel* (New York, 1965)

Rose, Jacqueline. *The Haunting of Sylvia Plath* (Cambridge, Mass., 1992)

Sands, Donald B. Ed. *Middle English Verse Romances* (re. 'The Wedding of Sir Gawain & Dame Ragnell') (Exeter, Neb., 1986)

Schmitz, Gotz. *The Fall of Women in Early English Narrative Verse* (Cambridge, 1990)

Strathern, Marilyn. *After Nature: English Kinship in the Late Twentieth Century* (Cambridge, 1992)

Turner, K. Ed. *I Dream of Madonna* (London, 1993)

Vidal-Naquet, Pierre. 'Slavery and the Rule of Women in Tradition, Myth and Utopia', in *Myth, Religion & Society*. Ed. R. L. Gordon. (Cambridge, 1981)

Welldon, Estela V. *Mother, Madonna, Whore: The Idealization and Denigration of Motherhood* (New York, 1992)

Wollen, Peter. 'Theme Park and Variations', *Sight & Sound,* Vol. 3, No. 7, July 1993, pp. 7–9

Zeitlin. Froma I. 'The Dynamics of Misogyny: Myth and Mythmaking in the "Oresteia" ', *Arethusa* Vol. 11, Nos. 1–2, Spring & Fall 1978, pp. 149–84

TWO

Balls, Edward & Gregg, Paul. *Work and Welfare: Tackling the Jobs Deficit* (London, 1993)

Bennett, G. & Smith, Paul. *Monsters with Iron Teeth: Perspectives on Contemporary Legend,* Vol. 3 (Sheffield, 1988)

Bly, Robert. *Iron John: A Book About Men* (Reading, Mass., 1990)

Dhubhne, Eilis Ni. ' "The Old Woman as Hare": Structure and Meaning in an Irish Legend' (re. 'The Robber that was Hurt'), *Folklore,* Vol. 104, Nos. 1–2, 1993, pp. 77–85

Gremaux, René. 'Mannish Women of the Balkan Mountains: Preliminary notes on the "Sworn Virgins" in Male Disguise, with Special Reference to their Sexuality and Gender Identity', in *From Sappho to De Sade: Moments in the History of Sexuality.* Ed. Jan Bremmer. (London & New York, 1989)

Gygax, Gary. *Official Advanced Dungeons & Dragons Monster Manual* 2 (Lake Geneva, Wis., & Cambridge, 1983)

Hudson, Liam & Jacot, Bernadine. *The Way Men Think: Intellect, Intimacy, and the Erotic Imagination* (New Haven, 1991)

MacKinnon, Catharine A. 'Crimes of War, Crimes of Peace', in *The Oxford Amnesty Lectures: on Human Rights.* Eds. Stephen Shute & Susan Hurley. (New York, 1993)

———. *Toward a Feminist Theory of the State* (Cambridge, Mass., 1991)

Parret, Herman; Verschaffel, Bart & Verminck, Mark. Eds. *Ligne, Frontière, Horizon* (Liège, 1993)

Phillips, Angela. *The Trouble with Boys* (New York, 1994)

Pitt-Rivers, Julian. *The Fate of Shechem or the Politics of Sex: Essays in the Anthropology of the Mediterranean* (Cambridge, 1977)

Samuels, Andrew. *The Political Psyche* (London, 1993)

Shelley, Mary Wollstonecraft. *Frankenstein*. Ed. Maurice Hindle. (Harmondsworth, 1992)

——. *The Last Man* (London, 1985)

Simpson, Jacqueline. 'Some Rationalized Motifs in Modern Urban Legends', *Folklore* Vol. 92, 1981, pp. 203–7.

Stoller, Robert. *Presentations of Gender* (London, 1992)

Strathern, Marilyn. *The Gender of the Gift: Problems with Women and Problems with Society in Melanesia* (London, 1988)

Topsell, Edward. 'The History of Four Footed Beasts & Serpents & Insects', taken from *Historiae Animulium* by Conrad Gesler (3 Vols.). Ed. Willy Ley. (London, 1967)

Turnbull, Don. Ed. *Fiend Folio: Tome of Creatures Malevolent and Benign* (Lake Geneva, Wis., 1981)

Twitchell, James B. *Preposterous Violence: Fables of Aggression in Modern Culture* (New York, 1989)

Ward, James & Kuntz, Rob. *Official Advanced Dungeons & Dragons: Legend & Lore* (Lake Geneva, Wis., 1984)

Zipes, Jack. 'Spreading Myths About Fairy Tales: a Critical Commentary on Robert Bly's "Iron John" ', in *Fairy Tales as Myth/Myth as Fairy Tale* (Lexington, Ky., forthcoming)

MISCELLANEOUS

Megapower Magazine, 2, September 1993; *Super Play,* 11 & 12, September–October 1993; *Sega Zone,* 11, September 1993; *Edge,* 3, December 1993; *Mega Sega Machines Amiga CD* (promotional materials).

THREE

Apuleius, Lucius. *The Golden Ass*. Trans. Robert Graves.(New York, 1973)

Barrie, James. *Peter Pan* (London, 1928)

Bettelheim, Bruno. *The Uses of Enchantment: the Meaning and Importance of Fairy Tales* (New York, 1978)

Boswell, John. *The Kindness of Strangers: the Abandonment of Children in Western Europe from Late Antiquity to the Renaissance* (New York, 1988)

Bottigheimer, Ruth B. *Grimm's Bad Girls and Bold Boys: The Moral and Social Vision of the Tales* (London, 1989)

Burkert, Nancy Eckholm. *Valentine and Orson* (New York, 1989)

Constantine, David. *Casper Hauser: a Poem in Nine Cantos* (London, 1994)

Dekker, Rudolf. *Out of the Shadow into the Light: Children in Egodocuments, 1600–1850* (Amsterdam, forthcoming)

Dekker, Rudolf & Limonard, Jurgen. 'The Diary of Alexander Van Goldstein (1801–1808): an Early "Adolescent Diary" ', *Paedagogia Historica*, Vol. 29, No. 1, 1993, pp. 151–64

Hills, John. *The Future of Welfare: a Guide to the Debate* (London, 1993)

Hughes-Hallett, Penelope. Ed. *Childhood: A Collins Anthology* (London, 1988)

Miller, Alice. *The Drama of Being a Child and the Search for the True Self*. Trans. Ruth Ward. (New York, 1988)

———. *Thou Shalt Not Be Aware; Society's Betrayal of the Child*. Trans. M. H. Mannum. (New York, 1985)

Rose, Jacqueline. *The Case of Peter Pan or the Impossibility of Children's Fiction* (London, 1994)

Tombeaux Romains. *Anthologie d'epitaphes latines*. Trans. Danielle Porte. (Paris, 1993)

Warner, Marina. 'Into the Dangerous World: Some Thoughts on Childhood and its Costs', *Counterblast* 5 (London, 1989)

Wasserman, Jakob. *Casper Hauser: the Inertia of the Heart*. Trans. Michael Hulse. (London, 1992)

Yule, Valerie. Ed. *What Happens to Children: the Origins of Violence* (Sydney, 1979)

FOUR

Beer, Gillian. *Forging the Missing Link: Interdisciplinary Stories* (Cambridge, 1991)

Bowler, Peter J. 'The Geography of Extinction: Biogeography and the Expulsion of "Ape Man" from Human Ancestry in the Early Twentieth Century', paper for *Pithecanthropus Centennial Symposium* (Leiden, 1993)

Carter, Angela. *The Bloody Chamber and Other Stories* (London, 1979)

Cavalieri, Paola & Singer, Peter. 'The Great Ape Project', paper for *Pithecanthropus Centennial Symposium* (Leiden, 1993)

Crankovich, Tony. ' "King Kong": Masterpiece of Adventure', *Classic Images,* No. 146, August 1987, pp. 15–17

Drake-Carnell, Francis. *It's an Old Scottish Custom* (re. 'Burry Man') (London, 1939)

Forbes Irving, P.M.C. *Metamorphosis in Greek Myths* (Oxford, 1992)

Gaignebet, Claude & Lajoux, Dominique J. *Art Profane et Religion Populaire au Moyen* (Paris, 1985)

Gilgamesh, The Epic of. Trans. N. K. Sandars. (Harmondsworth, 1960)

Goldner, Orville & Turner, George E. *The Making of 'King Kong'* (London & New York, 1975)

Greek Alexander Romance, The. Ed & trans. Richard Stoneman. (London, 1991)

Harryhausen, Ray. *Film Fantasy Scrapbook* (London, 1978)

Herbert, Zbigniew. *Still Life with Bridle* (London, 1993)

Husband, Timothy. *The Wild Man: Medieval Myth and Symbolism* (New York, 1981)

Jones, Malcolm. 'Wild Man'; 'Green Man', *Garland Encyclopaedia of Medieval Folklore* (New York, forthcoming)

Kightly, Charles. *The Customs and Ceremonies of Britain* (London, 1986)

Mayne, Judith. 'King Kong and the Ideology of Spectacle', *Quarterly Review of Film Studies,* Vol. 1, No. 4, November 1976, pp. 373–87

Montaigne, Michel de. *Essais.* Trans. John Florio, 1603. (London, 1946)

Oates, Caroline. 'Werewolves and Lycanthropy in Franche-Comté', in *Fragments for a History of the Human Body.* Eds. M. Feher, R. Naddaff, & N. Tazi *Zone,* Pt. 1, New York, 1989, pp. 305–63

Pieterse, Jan Nederveen. 'Apes Imagined: Notes on the Political Ecology of Animal Symbolism', paper for *Pithecanthropus Centennial Symposium* (Leiden, 1993)

Ritvo, Harriet. *The Animal Estate: the English and Other Creatures in the Victorian Age* (Harvard, 1987)

Rosen, David N. ' "King Kong": Race, Sex, and Rebellion', *Jump Cut,* March–April 1975, pp. 8–10

Snead, James. 'Spectatorship and Capture in "King Kong": the Guilty Look', *Critical Quarterly,* Vol. 33, No. 1, 1991, pp. 53–69

Thomas, Keith. *Man and the Natural World: Changing Attitudes in England 1500–1800* (Harmondsworth, 1984)

Valentine & Orson. From *Morris's Cabinet of Amusement and Institution* (London, 1822)

Valentine & Orson. *Aunt Primrose's Library* No. 8 (London, 1860)

Valentine & Orson. Trans. Henry Watson. Ed. Arthur Dickson. (Oxford, 1937)

FIVE

Appignanesi, Lisa & Forrester, John. *Freud's Women* (London, 1992)

Archibald, Elizabeth. *Apollonius of Tyre: Medieval and Renaissance Themes and Variations* (Cambridge, 1991)

Bouquet, Mary. *Man Ape, Ape Man: Pithecanthropus in Het Pesthuis* (Leiden, 1993)

Buchhorn, Richard. 'Ockam's Razor Talk', ABC Radio National, 26 July 1992

Dabydeen, David. *Turner: New and Selected Poems* (London, 1994)

Dudley, E. & Novak, M. E. 'The Wild Man Within: an Image in Western Thought', in *Renaissance to Romanticism* (Pittsburg, 1972)

European Parliament. Report Drawn Up On Behalf of the Committee of Inquiry on Racism and Xenophobia (Luxembourg, 1991)

Friedman, John. *The Monstrous Races in Medieval Art and Thought* (Harvard, 1981)

Gasper, Julia. *The Gynocratic Threat in 'The Tempest'* (kindly lent by the author)

Hulme, Peter. *Colonial Encounters: Europe and the Native Caribbean 1492–1797* (London, 1986)

Knutson, Roslyn L. *A Caliban in St Mildred Poultry* (Unpublished paper, University of Arkansas at Little Rock, 1992)

Kovel, Joel. *White Racism: a Psychohistory* (London, 1970)

Lee, Sir Sidney. 'Caliban's Visits to England', *The Cornhill Magazine,* Vol. 34, 1913, pp. 333–45

Morrison, Toni. *Playing in the Dark: Whiteness and the Literary Imagination* (Cambridge, Mass., & London, 1992)

Pagden, Anthony. *The Fall of Natural Man* (Cambridge, 1982)

Pieterse, Jan Nederveen. *White on Black: Images of Africa and Blacks in Western Popular Culture* (New Haven & London, 1993)

Rawson, Claude. 'Eating People', *London Review of Books,* 24 January 1985, pp. 20–2

———. 'Narrative and the Proscribed Act: Homer, Euripides, and the Literature of Cannibalism', in *Theory and Criticism: Festschrift in Honour of René Wellek,* Vol. 2, 1986, pp. 1159–87

———. 'Stewed, Roasted, Baked, or Boiled', *London Review of Books,* 6 August 1992, pp. 10–12

Ruskin, John. *Modern Painters* (Vol. 3) (London, 1842)

Shanes, Eric. *Turner* (London, 1993)

Vaughan, Alden T. & Vaughan, Virginia Mason. *Shakespeare's Caliban: a Cultural History* (Cambridge, 1991)

SIX

Anderson, Benedict. *Imagined Communities: Reflections on the Origin and Spread of Nationalism* (London, 1983)

Bann, Stephen. *The Inventions of History: Essays on the Representations of the Past* (Manchester, 1990)

Barnett, Anthony; Ellis, Caroline, & Hirst, Paul. Eds. *Debating the Constitution: New Perspectives on Constitutional Reform* (Cambridge, 1993)

Bhabha, Homi. Ed. *Nation and Narration* (London, 1990)

Brendon, Piers. *Our Own Dear Queen* (London, 1986)

Cannadine, David. *The Pleasures of the Past* (London, 1989)

Clifford, Sue & King, Angela. *Local Distinctiveness: Place, Particularity and Identity* (London, 1993)

Colley, Linda. *Britons: Forging the Nation 1707–1837* (New Haven & London, 1992)

Davies, Diana & Luard, Felicity. *Making and Meaning: the Wilton Diptych* (London, 1993)

Foster, R. F. *Paddy and Mr. Punch: Connections in Irish and English History* (London, 1993)

Furedi, Frank. 'The Politicisation of History in Post Cold War Europe', paper, *British Sociology Association Conference,* April 1992

Gilroy, Paul. 'Mixing It: How is British National Identity Defined? And How Do Race and Nation Intersect?', *Sight & Sound,* Vol. 3, No. 9, September 1993, pp. 24–5

Haskell, Francis. *History and its Images* (New Haven & London, 1993)

Ignatieff, Michael. *Blood and Belonging: Journeys into the New Nationalism* (London, 1993)

Kitaj, R. B. *First Diasporist Manifesto* (London, 1989)

Mulvey, Laura. 'Disgraced Monuments' (Channel 4 Film Documentary, forthcoming)

Naipaul, V. S. *The Enigma of Arrival* (London, 1987)

Nairn, Tom. *The Enchanted Glass: Britain and its Monarchy* (London, 1988)

National Curriculum. *History Working Group* (Department of Education and Science and the Welsh Office, 1989)

Rushdie, Salman. *Imaginary Homelands: Essays and Criticism 1981–1991* (London, 1991)

Stewart, Susan. *On Longing: Narratives of the Miniature, the Gigantic, the Souvenir, the Collection* (Durham & London, 1993)

Thatcher, Margaret. *The Downing Street Years* (London, 1993)

Townshend, Charles. *Making the Peace* (Oxford, 1993)

Walcott, Derek. *Collected Poems, 1948–1984* (London, 1992)

———. *Omeros* (London, 1990)

———. *The Odyssey. A Stage Version* (London, 1993)

Wollen, Peter. *Raiding the Ice Box: Reflections on Twentieth Century Culture* (London, 1993)

Wright, Patrick. *On Living in an Old Country: the National Past in Contemporary Britain* (London, 1985)

Young, James, E. *The Texture of Memory: Holocaust Memorials and Meanings* (New Haven & London, 1993)

Zipes, Jack. *The Brothers Grimm: From Enchanted Forests to the Modern World* (London, 1989)

Grateful acknowledgement is made to the following for permission to reprint previously published material:

Bloodaxe Books: Excerpt from *Caspar Hauser: A Poem in Nine Cantos* by David Constantine (Newcastle Upon Tyne: Bloodaxe Books, 1994). Reprinted by permission of Bloodaxe Books.

Jonathan Cape Ltd.: Excerpt from "Turner" from *Turner* by David Dabydeen (London: Jonathan Cape Ltd., 1994). Reprinted by permission of Jonathan Cape Ltd.

Farrar, Straus & Giroux, Inc.: Excerpt from "The Schooner Flight" from *Collected Poems 1948–1984* by Derek Walcott, copyright © 1986 by Derek Walcott. Reprinted by permission of Farrar, Straus & Giroux, Inc.

HarperCollins Publishers, Inc.: Excerpts from "Edge" and "Lady Lazarus" from *Ariel* by Sylvia Plath, copyright © 1963 by Ted Hughes, copyright renewed. Reprinted by permission of HarperCollins Publishers, Inc.

Rogers, Coleridge & White Ltd.: Excerpt from "The Tiger Bride" from *The Bloody Chamber* by Angela Carter (London: Victor Gollanz, 1979). Reprinted by permission of Rogers, Coleridge & White Ltd., London.

Virago Press Ltd.: Excerpt from "The Ubiquitous Lout" from *St. Suniti and the Dragon* by Suniti Namjoshi, copyright © 1994 by Suniti Namjoshi. Reprinted by permission of Virago Press Ltd., London.